NAPOLEON

Napoleon as a young officer (early or middle 1790s).

NAPOLEON

by Manfred Weidhorn

ATHENEUM ✾ 1986 ✾ NEW YORK

Excerpts from The Mind of Napoleon by J. Christopher Herold
reprinted by permission of the publisher.
© 1955, Columbia University Press

PICTURE CREDITS

French Cultural Services:
9, 16, 19, 22, 25, 73, 96–97, 109, 143, 198, 203
Musée Nationaux de France:
frontis, 2, 40–41, 57, 87, 92–93, 99, 121, 125, 173
Martial Achievements of Britain and Her Allies, London, 1815: 188–189

Atheneum
Macmillan Publishing Company
866 Third Avenue, New York, NY 10022

Type set by Maryland Linotype Composition Inc., Baltimore, Maryland
Printed and bound by Fairfield Graphics, Fairfield, Pennsylvania
Maps drawn & lettered by Bruce Hiscock
Designed by Marilyn Marcus

10   9   8   7   6   5   4   3   2   1

Library of Congress Cataloging in Publication Data

Weidhorn, Manfred.   Napoleon.

Bibliography: p. 206
Includes index.
SUMMARY: A biography of the military genius who crowned himself
Emperor of the French and whose empire covered most
of western and central Europe.
1. Napoleon I, Emperor of the French, 1769–1821—Juvenile literature.
2. France—Kings and rulers—Biography—Juvenile literature.
3. France—History—Consulate and Empire, 1799–1815—Juvenile literature.
[1. Napoleon I, Emperor of the French, 1769–1821. 2. Kings, queens, rulers, etc.
3. Generals. 4. France—History—1789–1815] I. Title.
C203.W38   1986   944.05′092′4   [92] 86-3352
ISBN 0-689-31163-X

TO

PHYLLIS
and our sons
ARON & ERIC

Contents

Preface   3

CHAPTER ONE
Young Man from Corsica (1769–1793)   5

CHAPTER TWO
General in Italy (1793–1797)   21

CHAPTER THREE
Adventurer in Egypt (1797–1799)   37

CHAPTER FOUR
First Consul in Paris (1799–1804)   48

CHAPTER FIVE
Emperor of the French (1800–1805)   62

CHAPTER SIX
The First Napoleonic War (1802–1807)   78

CHAPTER SEVEN
The Beginning of Resistance (1808–1809)   103

Contents

CHAPTER EIGHT
Indian Summer and Gathering Clouds (1809–1811)   116

CHAPTER NINE
The Moscow Trip (1812)   132

CHAPTER TEN
Closing the Ring (1813–1814)   157

CHAPTER ELEVEN
Elba, the Hundred Days, Waterloo (1814–1815)   175

CHAPTER TWELVE
St. Helena (1815–1821) and Beyond   192

Further Reading   206

Index   207

NAPOLEON

Preface

In 1819, British Archbishop Whately found his patience worn out. He was sick and tired of hearing from philosophers, skeptics, and atheists that the stories in the Bible, especially those involving miracles, are incredible and therefore fictitious. The archbishop believed that life itself is a miracle and that it is filled with many incredible characters and stories. He therefore set about writing a book that showed that the very arguments used to call into question the Biblical tales could be used to call into question as well the existence of living persons. To prove his point, he chose someone whose life and actions were so unbelievable that any reader with common sense would take the story to be an obvious piece of fiction, a far-fetched adventure novel. The individual he chose was the

Napoleon, Emperor of the French.

recent emperor of the French, and the title of his book was *Historic Doubts Relative to Napoleon Bonaparte*. This obscure but amusing volume establishes, more than does almost anything else, that Napoleon led one of the most exciting and legendary of all lives.

Here is the story of that life.

CHAPTER ONE

Young Man From Corsica

(1769–1793)

Winter snow lay on the beautiful and varied landscape, on fields and roads, on cities and towns of France, in early 1779. One of these towns, Autun, was a sleepy village with small cobbled streets, charming houses, and an old church. Near the center of town was the school, built centuries ago. It was recess time, and the sounds of children running, yelling, laughing, singing drifted down the quiet streets.

Yet not all was sweetness and light. Some of the children were standing in a semicircle in the schoolyard, and their attention was focused on a nine-year-old boy a few feet away. He was small and thin, with a large forehead, riveting eyes, finely shaped chin and nose, thin lips, and olive complexion. His clothes were somewhat shabby and foreign looking. The children were taunting him.

Napoleon at 14 (1783) by Pontornini. "My Dear Friend Buonaparte."
The earliest portrait of Napoleon by a contemporary.

Some imitated his manner of speaking badly broken French in a heavy Italianlike accent. Others made faces at him.

He wanted to hit them, but they were too many. He wanted very much to cry, but he would not let himself act like a girl or a sissy. He swallowed his tears and his pain. He was a boy newly arrived in the school and in the town, newly arrived even in the strange land called France, from his homeland Corsica. He felt lonely as he had never felt before and as, he was sure, no one else ever felt.

He looked again at the taunting, animallike faces. How he hated them! Some day, he told himself, some day he would show them how good he was. Some day, they would be sorry for their cruelty to him.

Many children have at one time or another felt such self-pity and then turned to other things without remembering their vows and promises to themselves. But this was different. Little did those schoolchildren know that boy's thoughts or how prophetic those thoughts proved to be. For this boy would someday rule not only over the schoolchildren—and their parents and their children—but over all the French people. This impoverished Corsican boy would someday become Emperor of the French and conqueror of nearly all Europe.

The name of this boy was Napoleon Buonaparte.

Napoleon was born on August 15, 1769, at Ajaccio on the Mediterranean isle of Corsica. The families of both his parents had come centuries earlier from northern Italy. His father, Carlo, belonged to the local aristocracy, such as it was. A worldly, intelligent, charming man who was fluent in French and Italian, he liked living in grand style even though he did not have much money. His extravagance revealed itself when he sometimes showed off expensive new clothing while his growing family went hungry.

So busy was he preening himself—and fighting for Corsican independence—that he left the upbringing of his many children to his wife, Letizia. Napoleon's mother was, unlike her husband, uneducated and tight-fisted with money. Although she was to know years of poverty, suffering, and hard work, she always remained a kind and loving person. Still, when she had to, she could be strict, something that Napoleon would always remember and respect. Even when her second son became emperor, she remained an unassuming woman whose simple, yet wise and prophetic words were, "If it would only last!"

7

The Corsicans had long struggled to achieve their independence. They had been oppressed by many peoples, the latest of whom were the Genoese. The fight against the Italian city-state of Genoa was being led by a Corsican military officer, Pasquale Paoli. All Europe watched and sympathized with their effort.

Just as Paoli's military campaign seemed to be succeeding, the Genoese, by a treaty in 1764, turned Corsica over to the French. Now the battle had to be resumed, this time with a much more powerful military foe. Sure enough, the French snuffed out Corsican resistance with ease by May 1769. Soon thereafter, while Carlo and Letizia, who had been involved in the struggle, were making their difficult way home from the last battlefield, Napoleon was born to them. Because of the French takeover, the infant was a French citizen at birth. Biologically and culturally, he was a Corsican. But, he was born at the beginning of the French possession of Corsica, and the gradual triumph of matters French over Corsican would be the pattern of the first phase of his life.

Carlo Buonaparte had been an ardent follower, even private secretary, of Paoli. When he saw, however, that the Corsican cause was lost, he quickly attached himself to the conquering French. Making many connections with the new rulers of the island, he got himself officially admitted as a member of the French nobility. When it was time for Napoleon's schooling, Carlo was therefore able to arrange to have the boy educated in France on a "scholarship" given by the king to aristocratic children—provided that the boy spoke French.

So it was that in early 1779 Napoleon was taken to the school in Autun to learn the French language. As a result of the teasing he ran into there, he was aware now, as never before, that he was a "Corsican," a despised member of a people considered inferior by the dominant French. His recourse was to daydream of his hero—the defeated leader of his people, the former chief of his father—Pasquale Paoli.

Napoleon as a schoolboy in a snowball fight (early 1780s).

Soon Napoleon knew enough French to be able to enter the Military Academy of Brienne. There he also ran into teasing, but now he had inner resources to fall back on. He began to read a lot, enjoying such subjects as history, geography, and military science. Consequently, he did very well on his examinations five years later (1784), and was recommended to the fashionable Ecole Militaire (Military School) at Paris, where he ran into more disdain, and this time snobbery as well. By now he had learned to take it—to convert the pain caused by taunting into independence, self-reliance, and manliness, rather

9

than letting it be an excuse for self-pity and daydreams. This character building was helped along by the school's tough military discipline and its emphasis on physical exercise.

The school accepted students from some of the best families in France and was well run. The impoverished young Napoleon was deeply impressed by the well-furnished rooms, the fine meals, the high quality of the teaching and of the supporting services. School had never been like this.

Unlike his docile older brother Joseph, Napoleon seemed to have been cut out for a career in the army: as a boy he was hot tempered, combative, and domineering; later, at the Military Academy of Brienne, when the pupils played soldier, he usually became the commander, sometimes of the attacking force, sometimes of the defense.

Then, in 1784, Carlo died, when only thirty-nine, leaving his wife with eight children to take care of and leaving Napoleon at fifteen without a role model and a guide and, of course, without money. Yet Napoleon appears to have already become self-directing and well motivated. He was a hard worker, and, in the fall of 1785, he was graduated from the military school after only one year of study instead of the normal two or three. Skipping over various ranks, furthermore, he was assigned as a second lieutenant to an artillery regiment.

A year later, he returned home for the first time in eight years, a proud young officer in a smart uniform and polished long boots, with sword and cocked hat. He was the seventeen-year-old Corsican who made good in the "big time" in France— the first Corsican, in fact, to have graduated from the prestigious Ecole Militaire. It was quite different from his status in France, where he was a poor, friendless foreigner without connections, and a far cry from the lonely nine year old taunted on that cold wintry day long ago.

His brothers and sisters crowded around him; his relatives and neighbors were impressed; the girls in town snuck admiring glances at him. He had come home like a conquering hero.

No wonder he enjoyed himself greatly there and obtained several extensions of his leave.

He read plays and history books. Taking pride in being an idealist and a lover of truth, he kept a thoughtful diary and began research for a projected history of Corsica. He did not rejoin his regiment in France for almost two years.

There, his general, seeing Napoleon's ability, placed him in temporary charge of two hundred men, to the audible annoyance of the senior officers. That was when Napoleon discovered that having a large group of strong young men in colorful uniforms march in formation in response to a few crisp words growled by him was one of the great mysteries and pleasures in life. The joy of leading and commanding was only equaled by the joy of solving problems in the use of force, in putting that colorful formation to work.

When a riot broke out in a small town, Napoleon was, despite his youthfulness, put in charge of a company of soldiers sent to establish order. Led by him, the soldiers arrived in town in smart order. But things soon became sticky. Litter and broken glass covered the main street, several houses were aflame —the smoke whipped up by the harsh March wind—and a mob of snarling, angry people was waiting. Napoleon's military schooling had dwelt mainly on the famous battles of the past, and not too much on crowd control in a French town, so he was on his own. He had the military firepower on his side, of course, and some of his fellow officers would have let that easy way out settle the matter right away. Napoleon, though, decided it would be better not to shed blood and not to have the other side lose face. But how?

He stepped in front of his men and addressed the menacing mob kept back only by the guns facing them. "My orders are to shoot the riffraff," he announced loudly, clearly, and confidently. "Those of you who are respectable town folk—as many of you seem to be—please leave now so as not to get caught in the crossfire with the riffraff." There was a moment of un-

EUROPE
1789

IRELAND

NORTH SEA

GREAT
BRITAIN

London ★

HOLLAND

BELGIUM

ATLANTIC OCEAN

★ Paris

FRANCE

SWITZE

Genc

Marseille
Toulon

CORSICA

Ajaccio

PORTUGAL

SPAIN

SARDINIA

MEDITERRANEAN

certainty and muttering. Then the crowd dispersed—for no one thinks of himself as riffraff! Napoleon winked at his men and posted his sentinels.

This civil disturbance was not accidental, for the year was 1789—one of the most fateful in world history.

Napoleon, we saw, had been born on Corsica, technically a French citizen but raised as a Corsican. Corsica was to France as Northern Ireland or Scotland is to England or Puerto Rico is to the U.S.: a small underdeveloped but proud country with its own culture but, because of its poverty and political weakness, dependent on a nearby large, powerful country. That dependence causes a "brain drain," as the best young people go to the larger country in order to make their careers there, and, unintentionally, thereby leave their own country even poorer. Napoleon was part of such a brain drain. He had been sent to obtain an education in a nearby land that was a center of world civilization, to make his way in the country where "the action was."

He might have led an obscure life in the French army were it not for a lucky stroke of history. For, despite being (along with England) the leading power in Europe, France was going through the greatest crisis of its life. The bonds of trust that held together king and people were, after years of rising tension, coming apart. The kings and their courtiers lived a life of extreme frivolity and luxury. They wasted large sums of money gathered through heavy taxes on the poor and oppressed French people. Wherever one went in city or countryside of this great nation, one saw hungry, miserable people and heard grumblings of resentment and hatred.

The handwriting was on the wall, but the ruling classes, instead of attending to the ills of the nation, distracted themselves with ever grander parties and forms of self-indulgence. There is a famous story that Queen Marie Antoinette, when told that the people had no bread to eat, callously replied, "Let them eat cake." Though the story is probably not true, it has received wide currency because it expresses so perfectly the indifference and irresponsibility of those at the top.

Not only the poor and the working classes, but also the prospering merchant or middle classes found themsleves shut out from political power. As a result, the large mass of the French population, regardless of income or rank, saw in the royal court the source of its frustrations. Working together, all segments of society insisted on having a larger role to play in government. They could get that only by taking away some of the power from the very small ruling group, which consisted of king, aristocracy, and church and which was answerable to no one. These few were not about to give up their privileges without a fight. The result was the Revolution of 1789, when the people finally asserted their rights by force.

Where did Napoleon stand in all this? His prime interests were his own career and the independence of Corsica. Still, living in France and wearing the uniform of a French soldier, he could not avoid becoming caught up in the storm and stress of the hour. In fact, being by chance in Paris in the summer of 1792, he witnessed one of the climaxes of the Revolution, for the anger of the people, at first directed mainly at the king's courtiers and ministers, now was vented on the king himself. They stormed the royal palace and slaughtered the King's Guard. The tumult, the rage, the sound of screaming, the faces distorted with hatred, the savage acts of killing and mutilation, the impotence of normal police forces, the panorama of men running around blindly, sometimes together like packs of wild beasts, sometimes individually like a neighborhood dog suddenly turned rabid—this frightening scene suggested to Napoleon that both rulers and ruled were at fault for allowing the situation to degenerate into chaos.

Napoleon, being a nobleman, had sympathy for the king. But he was also poor; he was a member of the artillery officer corps, which was more reform-minded than other parts of the officer class; and, above all, he was a proud Corsican seeking

Young Napoleon as an artillery officer (early 1790s).

independence for his land from the haughty French among whom he had to live and work. These facts of his life would incline him to favor any opening up of a rigid, oppressive society. So he sided with the French people against their king, even while having, as a disciplined soldier, a strong dislike of the unruly mob scenes that repeatedly punctuated the coming of violent change. It so happened that the tide of history was with the people rather than the king: Louis XVI was guillotined, and a republic was established. Perhaps Napoleon's choice of sides was dictated more by an ambitious man's intuition as to which side would win and would open careers to talent than by the idealist's abstract notions of right and wrong.

Home in Corsica in late September 1789, he wrote a reply to the Corsican aristocrats who had attacked the Revolution. He organized a local pro-Revolutionary militia. Later he got himself elected (by kidnapping his rival!) as second in command of a battalion of Corsican volunteers. The Revolution, furthermore, altered the status of Corsica from a colony to a department of France, giving Corsicans all the rights of Frenchmen. This change helped make Napoleon think like a Frenchman and like a revolutionary, especially when it came to grappling with local Corsican politics.

The Revolution had also made it possible for Paoli, the national hero, to return home from exile in England. In the festivities arranged for the occasion, Napoleon was selected to make the official speech welcoming Paoli back. He also continued his research on Corsican history and wrote essays on various philosophical subjects, including a rather pessimistic one on the nonmilitary, nonpolitical, nonhistorical subject of love. He even entered another of his essays (on happiness) in a contest; although it didn't win, it made an impression. Clearly, he had scholarly interests and a way with words.

In 1791, Napoleon was promoted to first lieutenant and sent to another regiment. When he came home once more on leave, he found himself caught up in the swirling Corsican politics. His former hero, Paoli, was turning out to have feet of clay. The Corsicans had idolized Paoli when he was, as the heroic loser against the powerful French, living far away in exile. But when he returned and became involved in partisan politics and bickering, he seemed to be just another politician. His pre-Revolutionary vision of politics suddenly seemed antiquated to many. The French mistrusted him from the start because he was conservative while the French government was moving leftward. And when in early 1793 war broke out between England and France, Paoli, who had been warmly received in England during his exile, could not even be relied on to side with the country of which he was now officially a citizen.

As for Napoleon, he shared in his countrymen's disillusionment with Paoli. He was, besides, by now more Frenchman than Corsican. And, more important, he was rapidly becoming ambitious, and one did not have to be a deep thinker to see that if you were going to make your mark in the world, turbulent and sophisticated France—especially when everything was becoming unhinged and fluid during a revolution—offered much wider prospects than that tight little island, which must have come to seem provincial and backward.

A series of events in 1792 and 1793 sorely strained relations between, on the one hand, the French government and Paoli and, on the other hand, between Napoleon and Paoli. The French attempted to conquer the adjacent island of Sardinia, and Napoleon—now a captain—led forces that brutally fired on civilians. Then Napoleon attempted to seize the Corsican citadel at Ajaccio. Paoli washed his hands of the whole Buonaparte family.

Things rapidly came to a dramatic climax in mid-1793. The French government ordered Paoli's arrest. The Corsicans rebelled against their French masters, and Paoli became hero and leader again. The houses of those prominent Corsicans who leaned toward the French were attacked and pillaged. The

Napoleon observes the capture of the royal Tuileries Palace by an enraged mob on 10 August 1792.

families were banished; their property was confiscated. Among these were the Buonapartes, who fled to the safety of France for good. Napoleon himself, it is reported, had to go into hiding and then make a daring escape by night.

The twenty-four-year-old Napoleon was now a Frenchman not only by uniform, speech, and modes of thought, but also by place of residence. His future lay in the army and in France rather than in the murky politics of little Corsica, where he had known mainly poverty, struggle, and defeat. His attitude was changing quickly in many ways. Not only was his allegiance to Corsica being replaced by allegiance to France and his patriotic devotion to Corsican independence being replaced by growing personal ambition, but his youthful idealism and love of truth were being replaced by a growing realism or cynicism about people as they were. On his deathbed, he reminisced: "In my youth, I had illusions. I got rid of them fast." After watching the Revolutionary bloodshed in Paris in 1792 and expressing to a brother his contempt for all parties to the conflict for letting things unravel this far, he made an observation that sounds particularly disconcerting coming from a sympathizer of the Revolution: "The people are not worth the trouble taken in winning their favor."

CHAPTER TWO

General in Italy

(1793 – 1797)

With the execution of King Louis XVI in 1793, the reformers and radicals were firmly in control of France. But the nation faced an external threat from an outraged Europe, from a collection of insecure monarchs eager to mount a crusade against the Revolution and republicanism. Full-scale war broke out.

In the fall of 1793, a British fleet in the Mediterranean Sea joined with Spanish and French Royalist land forces to seize the major naval base of Toulon in the south of France. This was an important move in an attempt to recapture France for the Bourbons, the French royal family. The French Revolutionary government immediately sent an army unit to the scene. Napoleon, a captain of artillery in nearby Marseilles, was offered command of the artillery in the Toulon operation. He would be acting lieutenant colonel. At last he had a position in which his military ability could be tested.

Napoleon at the Battle of Toulon, 1793.

Napoleon rushed to the city and threw himself into the challenge. The key to the problem seemed to be the British fleet's possession of the inner harbor. But ejecting the big ships with their powerful guns would be no easy matter. Still, he thought something could be achieved if firepower were brought properly to bear on the enemy-held forts situated on a promontory between the inner and outer harbor.

Accordingly, Napoleon evolved a battle plan and presented it to his superiors. They gave him a free hand in artillery matters, and he ordered the cannons moved to the area of the forts, concentrating the firepower. His excellently positioned cannons scored direct hits. The forts surrendered. The British ships, coming under fire now from the forts and the cannons, retreated. The infantry and cavalry then overwhelmed the enemy's land forces, and Toulon fell.

For this achievement, Napoleon received high praise from various influential men. On the strength of his role in the capture of Toulon, he was made brigadier general and, soon thereafter, general of artillery in the Army of Italy. Such quick promotion was not unusual in an army that had a large turnover because of deaths during the current wars and, especially, the ouster of officers associated with the "old regime" of the former king, Louis XVI. In getting this post, Napoleon was helped by his considerable talent, by a series of lucky events, and, not least, by his contacts. Actively supporting the radical party in power, he had as sponsor, or patron, the brother of the Dictator Robespierre.

That very backing suddenly turned into a liability when, in the turmoil of French politics of the period, the dictator fell from power and was executed. Napoleon found himself arrested. But as there was no real evidence against him and as his military talent was needed by the Republic, he was soon free.

He had not yet found his destiny. The brief imprisonment was only one of several detours at this period. His participation in a French attempt to reconquer his native, rebellious Corsica came to nothing. He had to pretend to be ill in order to dodge assignment away from Paris; he was not about to go to a front (fighting reactionary peasants in the west of France) and to a military branch (infantry) which he disliked. He made a plan of campaign for the French forces in Italy, but, although the politicians approved it, the military authorities did not. Despite these various setbacks, he was catching the attention of prominently placed people. He seemed to be a military man of rare ability, especially after his disposition of artillery helped rout an Austrian force in September 1794.

An incident then occurred which did for his political career what Toulon had done for his military one. When the ruling faction in the Convention (or legislature) passed an edict stating that two-thirds of its own members had to sit in any future assembly, certain districts of Paris turned against the government. An insurrection was brewing.

Late in an evening of October 1795, a meeting took place in a conference room of one of the old Parisian royal palaces now serving as a government office building. Grim-faced politicians, members of the latest executive branch, the Committee of Five Directors, were seated around a table immersed in long discussions. The problem was the rising constitutional crisis. The present government, trying to consolidate its power, had found instead that their actions had aroused the people. Because of the incompetence of the general in charge of the soldiers in Paris, General Buonaparte was sent for.

Hours went by, and no decision was arrived at. Napoleon sat in a corner of the room listening to it all and periodically glancing at the clock. Taking the measure of each politician, he arrived at no high estimation of them. They were really not that much different from the populace rampaging outside. They were frightened, concerned only with their own interests, and confused.

As dawn arrived, the incoming bulletins became worse. Finally, the politicians had no choice but to turn the matter over to the military and make Napoleon commander of all troops in Paris. They urged him to refrain from violence.

Napoleon, conscious that time had just about run out, excused himself for his brusqueness and said, "Are you waiting for the people to give you permission to fire on them?"

He was curtly dismissed with the order he had been waiting for: to do whatever he felt necessary.

Napoleon's troops, thanks to his readiness to use his well-placed cannons on the mob leaders, quickly won the brief battle in the Paris streets. He thereby found sudden prominence as

The Committee of Public Safety appoints Napoleon Commander in Chief of the Army of the Interior, 1795.

25

the savior of the current government. He was made major general and then, although only twenty-six years old, commander in chief of the Army of the Interior. Throwing himself wholeheartedly into his new job, he improved the fighting quality of the forces under his command and established his popularity with the interest he took in bettering the lives of the soldiers. Soon he was to be given an even more challenging command.

While attending to the needs of the army and the country, he also took care of his family. It was not long before he was able to send his mother large sums of money—no questions were asked as to where he got it—and he saw to it that his brothers and his kinsmen from Corsica received good schooling or jobs.

He made arrangements for his own private life as well. In 1794, he had been close to marrying a sixteen-year-old girl in Marseilles. But now he was attracted to Josephine de Beauharnais, who came from a prominent family in the West Indies, and who had barely missed losing her life during the Revolutionary Reign of Terror. She had become part of Parisian high society, where beautiful women mingled with prominent politicians. She was seven years older than he, a widow, and the mother of two children. They were married in March 1796, and two days later he had to leave for the headquarters of the French Army of Italy. She remained in Paris leading a fashionable life, so that while he was piling up his military victories, he also was periodically melancholy over rumors of her unfaithfulness back home.

Napoleon at this time, when he was first making his mark in Parisian military, political, and social circles, was not a particularly impressive-looking person. Rather short (his height is variously given as five feet two inches or five feet six inches), he was also very thin. His hair was done in an unfashionable style; his face was not notably handsome; his skin was olive-colored. Yet people were struck by his broad forehead, his quick movements, and his alert eyes. His nimble mind and his ability to converse on many topics gave him an air of authority, whether in dealing with fellow officers or with his political bosses in Paris, the Directory. Self-conscious about his origins, he hated to be called or thought of as "the Corsican." In order to be "absolutely French," he changed his name from the Italianate "Buonaparte" to the French "Bonaparte."

By virtue of his growing influence and of his plan for the conduct of the Italian campaign, Napoleon was next made general of the Army of Italy—that is, the French army stationed in Italy. His mission was to carry out the plan of campaign he himself had submitted two years earlier—a double triumph, showing that, in the eyes of prominent people, he had a head on his shoulders and the ability to carry ideas out.

Or was someone trying to do him in? The Army of Italy had done little creditable work in four years. Beset by terrible problems of morale, lacking in food, supplies, and discipline, placed in an awkward strategic position, it was the worst French army at this time. If this was a trick, Napoleon was not worried. He held himself to the highest standards: "Either I shall restore order or I shall cease to command these bandits." He proceeded to work day and night in overhauling and reorganizing the army, in making "terrifying examples" of looters and other irresponsible elements.

His achievement can best be gauged by the results on the battlefield, for the campaign in Italy proved to be nothing less than spectacular, even unique. A dozen victories in as many months made him a superstar overnight. Here was a breakthrough for France and, above all, for himself. He did this, in part, by promising the soldiers everything—and coming through: "Soldiers! You are ill-fed and almost naked. I shall lead you into the most fertile plains on earth. There you shall find great cities and rich provinces. There you shall find honor, glory, riches."

The monarchies of Europe had been at war with Revolutionary France since 1792. The enthusiastic citizen armies of France, fighting on behalf of their nation and of the principles of the Revolution, had had great success against the traditional armies fighting more for pay than for the kings who hired them. Several nations dropped out of the conflict. Now, in 1796, only Britain, Austria, and Piedmont remained in the war. Piedmont, in northern Italy, was a sort of possession of the Austrian Empire, and the French and Austrians had turned it into a battlefield.

Napoleon's plan was to separate the Austrians and Piedmontese and then drive the Austrians out of Italy. A great and simple idea, but who would do it and how? One of Napoleon's many talents lay in moving armies about quickly, selecting the foe's vulnerable point, and massing artillery fire against it before sending in the infantry and cavalry forces. Another specialty of his was to catch the enemy with its forces divided or to compel it to divide its forces. Then, with his own massed power, he would fight the separated forces one at a time, so that in any battle he usually had a numerical superiority of troops. In that way, he could destroy the enemy, piece by piece.

His campaign was also marked by great coordination and unprecedented speed. Making his preparations carefully, he often won the battle before the armies even appeared in the field. As he liked to put it, by taking all factors into account, he forced luck to favor him. To this mastery of strategy must be added his determination, his eloquence in stating the goals of a campaign, and his air of authority. He had that rare personal magnetism that persuaded soldiers to lay down their lives for him. He was young, smart, energetic, sure of himself; in short, a natural leader. Now, at last, he had a campaign of his own to lead.

In April 1796, the Austrians, thinking they still faced a disorganized, demoralized French army, took the offensive in the Piedmont. In a series of six battles in less than three weeks, they consistently and completely lost to the superior strategy and tactics of the French General Bonaparte. Something new had entered the European stage, though few realized it yet. Among those few may have been the Piedmontese. They promptly got out of the war, making peace with the French at the price of surrendering various districts and large sums of money.

The Directors in Paris became nervous that Napoleon's success would make him too powerful and proposed to divide his command, but General Bonaparte threatened to resign. He had established his credentials and now shrewdly translated his military achievements into political capital. He also knew that, in dealing with the civilian chiefs at home, a positive approach was as helpful as a negative one of threats, bluffs, and ulti-matums. Therefore, when a victory brought about the fall of a city or province, he forced on the losers a peace treaty that extracted from them large sums of money, as well as—since he was an educated, somewhat cultivated person—valuable manu-scripts and works of art. Keeping a healthy bundle for himself, he despatched the bulk to his chiefs in Paris. Sending the loot home freed him from having to treat the suspicious and greedy politicians with any deference, as they needed him more than he needed them.

Once Piedmont was subdued, Napoleon turned his atten-tion to the main Austrian force in Italy. He sent proclamations to the Italian people, urging them to greet the French army as their liberators. The French people, he claimed, were not fight-ing the Italian people but the tyrants in Italy, even as they had overthrown the tyrants in Paris. It was part of Napoleon's genius to see, as do few generals and politicians, that military and political considerations cannot be separated. War is not kind to specialists, experts, men of limited vision. Unlike the cau-tious souls of the Directory, with their limited war aims, he saw war as being total. It involved men's heads and hearts as well as their hands and purses. The weapon of ideology and idealism had been handed down to him by the revolutionaries,

Napoleon at the bridge in the Battle of Arcole, 1796 (detail). When the French troops were repulsed, Napoleon seized the standard and rushed forward, yelling: "Soldiers! Aren't you the heroes of Lodi? Follow me!" Painted soon after the incident.

but he used it to better military effect. In his exploitation of popular enthusiasm for liberty and reform, he was one of the founders of modern propaganda.

\The Austrians retreated before this combined military and political offensive, still not knowing that they were up against a new kind of force. Napoleon went in hot pursuit. He won an important victory at a bridge in Lodi in May 1796 which, he later said, first gave him the sense that he was a "superior man." He began to think big now. He wanted to drive the Austrians out of Italy altogether and then join his army with the French Army of the Rhine in an invasion of Germany. /

In quick time, Napoleon had revolutionized the war in Italy. When he had taken over, it had been a diversion, an attempt by the French to harass the Austrian's military left wing, to distract attention from the main front in Central Europe. He had turned the war in Italy into an end in itself, into a main front with great possibilities.

Napoleon next occupied Milan, the prosperous capital of Austrian Lombardy. Here, he was welcomed by the ecstatic population as a conquering hero, a guardian of their liberties against the Austrians. Half of Italy had been won by the French in quick time, and the Austrians were in full retreat. Though he was to achieve bigger things, Napoleon later believed that this was his happiest period, perhaps because success was a new thing to him. "What enthusiasm! What shouting- 'Long live the liberator of Italy!' At 25[26]!" He felt like a superman or a god: "Already I felt the earth flee from beneath me, as if I were being carried to the sky."

Napoleon next besieged Mantua and repelled no less than four strenuous Austrian attempts to relieve the city and lift the siege. In July 1796, with Napoleon still busy at Mantua, the Austrian Emperor Francis met with his ministers and generals. Napoleon's victories in Italy had become a potential embarrassment for Austria. After much deliberation over the matter, the emperor decided to stick it out. He sent one of Austria's leading military men, Count Wurmser, with a large army to drive the French out of Italy.

The new Austrian move was so serious that Napoleon had to raise the almost-concluded siege at Mantua and concentrate on winning in the field instead. That was smart thinking. Beating an army always takes priority over capturing a city, no matter how large, important, or famous. A fallen city, as Napoleon himself was to learn to his chagrin in Russia many years later, is an empty triumph if the enemy army is still a threat. But once the army in the field is beaten, the defenseless city falls automatically.

Napoleon proceeded to give Wurmser a severe drubbing. The Austrians thereupon sent two more armies to Italy. In November 1796, Napoleon attacked one of them from the rear and defeated it at a bridge in the village of Arcole. This was one battle where he made a bad start. He had a close call, and his losses were heavy. Still, he was the victor in the end, and, as an extra reward, the victory sealed the fate of besieged Mantua.

When Napoleon scored yet another big victory, at Rivoli in January 1797, the Emperor Francis of Austria again met with his ministers and generals. After agonizing discussions, it was decided to make one last try for success by sending the emperor's brother, the Archduke Charles, to Italy. The emperor did not get along too well with his brother, but the archduke happened to be the best military brain Austria had at this time and he had been victorious against the French on other fronts. If anyone could stop the rampaging beast, the archduke could.

Not one to back down from challenges, Napoleon started a new offensive. This one sent the archduke reeling and brought the French to within sight of Vienna, the capital of the Austrian Empire. But, because of the uncertain military and political situation confronting him, Napoleon called for peace talks. His genius included the ability to know—at least until late in his career, when his inspiration left him—when to stop, when not to take unnecessary risks. As he so poetically put it, "I was play-ing at Twenty-One [Blackjack], and I held at Twenty."

Now Napoleon shifted gears. To traditional diplomacy, he brought the missionary zeal of the French Revolution, his own brilliant mind, and his military achievements. Generals are good at winning battles, but then have to watch the politicians negotiate away at the table what has been won on the field. Politicians have great ideas but are dependent on generals who are often incompetent as politicians. Whether as general or diplomat, Napoleon had to depend only on himself—and what a self! His generalship aided his diplomacy greatly, for the Austrians knew that if he did not get what he thought was fair he would simply resume hostilities. His own battlefield vic-tories established the terms of his peace treaties. As an excellent negotiator, he now played a major role in the first of many peace treaties he coauthored and signed, the Treaty of Campo Formio (October 1797) between the French Republic and the Austrian Empire. A very important clause in it established, in Italian territories conquered by the French, a new state. This Cisalpine (South of the Alps) Republic was made up of the most flourish-ing north Italian cities that had been ruled by kings and dukes. The constitution of this republic, drawn up by Napoleon, was modeled on that of Revolutionary France.

The conservative Austrian government and its emperor had to agree most reluctantly to something unheard of. It was no longer a case of one country beating another and then taking away some of the loser's land and money but leaving the government and society intact. The victor was now imposing a new—and threatening—form of government. Napoleon was exporting the French Revolution; he was behaving like a radical general and, at this stage of his career, probably doing so sincerely.

He was turning out to be not just a tough diplomat but also a shrewd politician abroad as well. He had always been as interested in political as in military matters. Now he did not

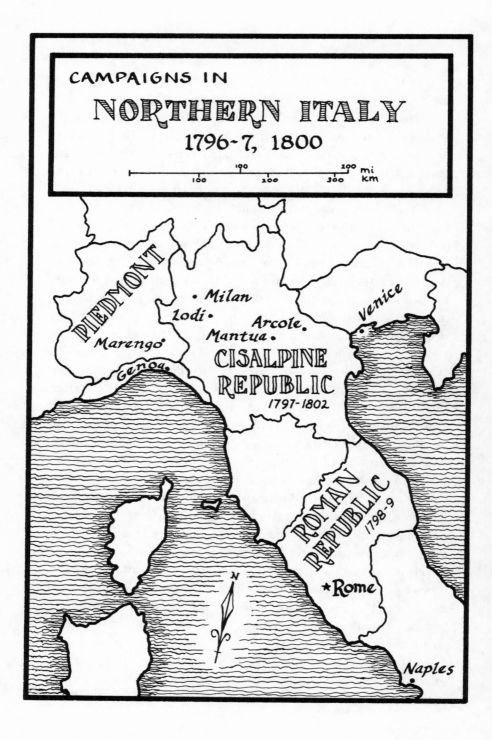

CAMPAIGNS IN
NORTHERN ITALY
1796-7, 1800

100   200 mi
100 200 300 km

PIEDMONT

• Milan
Lodi •   Arcole
Mantua •   •

Venice

Marengo •

Genoa •

CISALPINE
REPUBLIC
1797-1802

ROMAN
REPUBLIC
1798-9

N

★ Rome

Naples
•

stop with signing a peace treaty and establishing a new state and a new system of government. Even more striking—and ominous for the future of France and of Europe—he was beginning to play a leading part in the day-to-day running of this new country. Although the constitution provided for democratic institutions, Napoleon took it upon himself to personally organize the government and to appoint the ministers, legislators, and judges. He was the whole show behind the scenes.

The original war aims of the Directory had been to secure the "natural frontiers" of France—the Alps and Pyrenees mountains and the Rhine River—but Napoleon had virtually annexed northern Italy to France. As long as he had the Army of Italy behind him, the force that he had single-handedly turned into a sharp sword, who would talk back to him—the floundering Austrians? the liberated, hero-worshipping Italians? the far-off, eclipsed politicians of the Directory in Paris?

Napoleon, in short, was, in 1797, flowering on many sides at the same time: as military commander, as diplomat, as constitution maker, as ruler of much of northern Italy, as politician and administrator. At a mere twenty-eight, he had made himself the center of French and European politics. Not since Alexander the Great and Julius Caesar in the ancient world had anyone so versatile appeared in Western civilization and at such a young age. Besides, Alexander and Caesar had had the advantage of coming from prominent families, whereas Napoleon came from obscure, or at least impoverished, origins and was even initially an alien in France.

Great men always arouse hatred and envy. Although the French people admired Napoleon's feats and reveled in the spread of their Revolutionary institutions, his political bosses in Paris, the Directors, were unhappy. They were being overshadowed by their employee, by his personal management of the peace talks at their expense, by his growing military power and quickly spreading popularity. They, no less than foreign kings, found him to be a force to reckon with. For his part,

Napoleon was contemptuous of them. Sensing that he, not they, was in tune with the people, he had no fear of the Directory.

Having defeated the Austrian armies, Napoleon now turned his attention to other unfinished business in Italy. By means of an ultimatum, he forced Venice, a once-powerful city-state, to turn its traditional oligarchy (rule by the few) into a French-style republic. The new government promptly called in the French troops and ended Venice's proud independence. A similar transformation under French—that is, Napoleon's— "encouragement" occurred within days in the prominent city-state of Genoa, the former oppressor of Corsica. The Duke of Tuscany and even the pope were forced by Napoleon to sue for peace and to pay for it in the usual way with large sums of money, works of art, and manuscripts.

While immersed in all this political-diplomatic intrigue, Napoleon for a while set up residence in a castle in Milan. Attracting diplomats and tourists from all over Italy, it soon came to seem like the residence of a king. As a brilliant general, a statesman governing northern Italy, and a diplomat negotiating a favorable peace with the powerful Austrian Empire, he had become a celebrity.

A question begins to loom large. Whom was he ultimately working for—France or himself? There may not be any simple answer. Perhaps he worked for both simultaneously. One historian said that Napoleon combined the principles of the French Revolution with a personal lust for conquest, the reform spirit and missionary zeal of his age and of his country with the need to be the one to spread it. Even to his contemporaries he was an enigma. More and more people were saying about him something like what one French general had said as early as 1793: "You ask me what is this General Bonaparte? To know what he is, one would have to be he."

CHAPTER THREE

Adventurer
in Egypt
(1797–1799)

While Napoleon was gobbling up Italy for France, the Royalists (the followers of the overthrown king) tried in September 1797 to recapture power in Paris. Keeping his senses attuned to developments at home, the politically alert Napoleon promptly threatened to bring the Army of Italy right into Paris from its battle positions. To show that he meant business, he sent one of his generals to the French capital. That quickly quieted things down. Thus, for the second time, he saved the Revolution. He also thereby further introduced the army, and himself, into politics.

When he returned to the capital in December, Napoleon was acclaimed by delirious crowds as a national hero—and with reserve by the Directors. The Directors had to swallow their suspicions and consult with him on foreign policy matters. In a speech, he proclaimed the era of representative government, this great idea, which Revolutionary France had the honor of giving to all Europe. Acquaintances encouraged him to enter politics, but that same intuition and self-restraint that worked so well for him in military matters, that kept him from marching prematurely on to Rome and to Vienna, now told him that his hour in Paris had not yet come.

During his stay in Paris, he steered clear of politics and, living in semiseclusion, he immersed himself in conversations on learned topics with scientists and scholars. Always interested in intellectual matters, he seemed to know something about everything. He was even made a member of the academic Institute of France.

With Austria out of action, the only one of the original six enemies of Revolutionary France left was Britain, which, with its superior fleet, had inflicted several defeats on the French. His phenomenal success in Italy forced the Directory to appoint Napoleon commander of the newly formed Army of England and to give him the task of invading the island nation. As a good republican, he thought, like the others, that the British monarchy must be overthrown for the security of France and the welfare of Europe.

A few days after turning his attention to the challenges of an overseas invasion, Napoleon produced a plan. On personally inspecting the ports from which an armada was to be launched, however, he changed his mind. The difficult and dangerous project could not be carried out until France obtained command of the seas, something that would take years. He suggested instead a move into the Middle East to strike at Britain's lifeline with India. He may even have dreamed of the conquest of India itself, a goal that had lured Alexander the Great as well.

In the fall of 1797 and the spring of 1798, Napoleon presented formal proposals for an expedition to Egypt. The idea was not new, for Egypt had long seemed to Europeans to be an ageless, exotic place, but only Napoleon had put together a concrete plan of action. The Directory, perhaps thinking that far-off Egypt would do a better job of burying Napoleon than had the Army of Italy, agreed. It was for them a no-lose situation: if he succeeded, Egypt would be a nice jewel for the French to possess, and if he lost, they would be rid of a dangerous rival. Preparations began immediately.

In May 1798, a fleet of four hundred ships left France, the largest armada in the Mediterranean since the Crusades some five hundred years earlier. The first stop was Malta, which was second only to Gibraltar as an island fortress and which Napoleon had declared to be of great strategic value. The rulers of Malta, surrendering after a token resistance, provided large funds to Napoleon. With a series of administrative orders, he proceeded—in a week!—to reorganize and modernize the island, once again turning a feudal society into a French-style republic.

Resuming the expedition, the fleet arrived at the old Egyptian metropolis of Alexandria. The city fell almost at once. Most of the army then set off by land for Cairo. This march in the grueling Egyptian sun turned out to be terrible. Some men died of thirst, hunger, heat; others killed themselves to end their suffering. Before finally fighting a battle at Gizeh within sight of the fabled pyramids, Napoleon said to his men, "Soldiers, forty centuries have their eyes upon you!" After an easy victory, the French occupied Cairo.

At this point, Napoleon was beginning to realize that he was in the same league with Alexander the Great and Julius Caesar, two giants of history who also passed through the exotic Middle East on the way to bigger things. "Then indeed I felt I could abandon myself to the most brilliant dreams."

Napoleon settled in the Egyptian capital for the second half of 1798 and saw to the occupation and reorganization of the rest of the country. Taking taxation and agriculture, in particular, under his control, he established the basis for a modern society in Egypt. Free from the interference of faraway Paris, he could act like an all-powerful sultan. He instituted a

Divan General or Assembly of Notables modeled on some
French Revolutionary experiments in government.

Napoleon's policy was to achieve a cultural fusion—or, if
you will, to sow the seeds of an enlightened brand of modern
imperialism in Africa. He wanted the Moslem authorities to

The Battle of the Pyramids at Gizeh, 1798.

declare that swearing allegiance to the French was not inconsistent with their Moslem religion. And to humor the beliefs
of the natives, he acted as though the French army would convert to Islam. In his appeal to the troops, he urged them to
respect the different customs of the Moslems and warned them

41

against rape and looting. He tried to present the French and the Revolution they stood for as not inconsistent with Islam, and he offered to have French troops protect the pilgrims to Mecca. He participated in religious celebrations of the birthday of Mohammed and, for a while, even dressed—as had Alexander the Great—like a native.

As far as Napoleon was concerned, the French were in Egypt not only to cripple Britain, but also with the nonmilitary goals of spreading European values abroad and studying Egyptian antiquity. He therefore took with him hundreds of scholars and scientists (including a poet and a composer—early versions of our public relations experts). On the trip over, he had spent his time with the scholars, to the mystification and derision of his generals. Once in Egypt, these scholars laid the foundations for modern Egyptology (the study of Egyptian culture) and the scientific basis for what was to be the Suez Canal. Among other things, they discovered the Rosetta stone, which led to the deciphering of ancient hieroglyphic writing.

Having in this way introduced Egypt to Western civilization, and Europe to the study of ancient Egypt, Napoleon was made vice-president of the newly formed Institute of Egypt and even participated in some of its meetings. He thought so highly of the intellectual side of the expedition that he signed himself as "Member of the Institute" alongside "Commander in Chief."

Napoleon wanted the Egyptians—and the Turks who governed them by proxy—to believe that the war was against neither the Turkish Ottoman Empire nor the Islamic faith, but against the reactionary Mameluke beys, feudal military despots who ruled Egypt. The Turks were hardly persuaded, as they soon showed, for Napoleon's successes in Egypt were undone by two predictable events: a British naval victory and a falling out with Turkey.

During his stay in Cairo, Napoleon received news of a terrible setback. While crossing the Mediterranean, the French armada had been lucky not to run into the British war fleet which, under Admiral Nelson, was patroling the sea. The two forces had barely missed each other several times. Then Nelson finally caught up with the French fleet as it was anchored in Aboukir Bay near Alexandria. With the daring for which the British navy, and especially Nelson, were famous, the British destroyed the French fleet in what was so far the biggest victory of the war between the two nations. At one stroke, the British seized control of the Mediterranean, cut off the Army of Egypt from France, aborted any dream Napoleon may have had of continuing on to India, quickened Turkey's declaration of war against France, and made possible the formation of a new alliance against the French.

The Turkish declaration of war caused an uprising in Cairo against the French by people sympathetic to the Turks. Napoleon was quick to put it down and to have its leaders beheaded on successive days in order to strike fear and obedience into the populace. He was lenient as a matter of policy, but in the face of insurrection or betrayal, policy dictated ruthlessness. Obedience, he believed, came only from fear.

Though the morale of the French soldiers was sinking and his own position in Egypt was imperiled by events, Napoleon betrayed no emotion on hearing of the naval defeat at Aboukir or the insurrection in Cairo. He remained confident about the pace of progress in the conquest of upper Egypt and about the eventual outcome of things. Turkey's entry into the war gave him the idea of—or the excuse for—striking hard at her. If he could not go to India, he could at least go to Syria (another Turkish possession). Such a move would secure the French conquest of Egypt, cripple the supply lines of the British Mediterranean fleet, and, perhaps most inspiringly, liberate the Syrians from their local tyrant even as Napoleon had liberated the Italians from the Austrians and the Egyptians from the Mamelukes.

The French army proceeded to the area of Syria known as Palestine (and today Israel). There it captured Jaffa. The soldiers, who were in no mood for the Syrian campaign, rampaged through the conquered town, killing many civilians. Discipline was breaking down and Napoleon did not help matters when he added to the wanton bloodshed; lacking facilities for handling the 3,000 Turkish prisoners of war, he ordered them, against all Western tradition, to be slain.

The army then marched north to Acre. If Napoleon expected a repeat of the easy conquest of Jaffa, he was in for a surprise. The place was well fortified and, thanks to the cunning use of seapower by a British fleet, held out successfully. Meanwhile a Turkish army was coming down from Damascus. This rescue force was easily and brilliantly defeated by Napoleon near Mount Tabor.

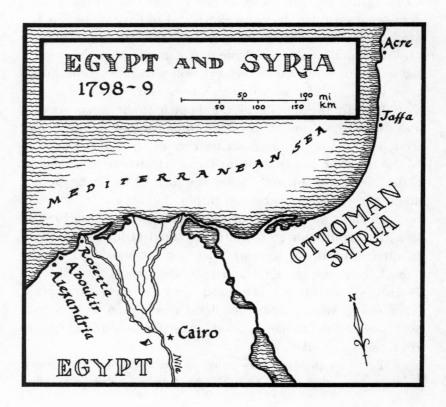

Acre, however, continued to hold out. Back in Egypt, another insurrection, this time led by a religious zealot, had to be put down in Napoleon's absence. Then the plague began to spread among the French soldiers at Acre. Napoleon was always a man for quick offensive action in the field and not drawn-out siege operation, and so, when the French army reached the limit of its endurance, he decided to forestall a mutiny and to give up the siege. This was the first military failure in his career. It ended, at least for then, any ambitious plans he may have had for going deeper into Asia, perhaps to Constantinople (Istanbul). As the retreat to Egypt began, he ordered that French soldiers felled by the plague, who could neither recover nor return, be given poison lest they fall into the hands of the vindictive natives.

The return of Napoleon to Egypt helped matters a little, but enemy armies were still harassing the French, and troop morale was still terrible. Now a new Turkish army came from the island of Rhodes and landed at Alexandria. Napoleon rushed to meet it, and his disposition of the forces is a show-case of military strategy. On July 25, 1799, the French attacked and won a brilliant victory at Aboukir, entirely destroying a Turkish force twice the size of the French. The sight of many enemy soldiers drowning while trying to get away "was the most terrible I ever saw." But winning made it "one of the most beautiful battles I ever saw."

Napoleon returned to Cairo and decided that, under the circumstances, there was far more for him to accomplish in Europe than in Egypt. He was not one to be sultan of a semi-pacified underdeveloped country, especially when things were happening fast in Europe. Russia and Turkey had declared war on France; Naples and Austria were on the move; a grand alliance, the most powerful France had yet faced, was being formed; in June, two French armies had been defeated within days, in Italy and on the Rhine; Italy, the country he had conquered so sensationally in a year of hard campaigning, had now been lost by lesser generals in a mere month of blundering military actions. No wonder Napoleon felt the urge to leave Egypt.

On August 24, 1799, Napoleon, with only some of his leading generals and followers, left Alexandria and barely slipped past the cruising British ships. The Directory had been getting ready to recall him with his army, not without it. Some in the government wanted him arrested for deserting his men and his post. To many in Napoleon's army and officer circle, it seemed that he had indeed abandoned the men who had fought so hard for him. What had begun gloriously ended with a sudden flight, as would happen again years later in Russia.

Viewed broadly, the Egyptian campaign, unlike the recent Italian one, was in many ways absurd. It was the product of a swollen romantic imagination, of childish fantasies, of personal vanity. Despite its impact on the imagination of Europe, on a sleepy Egyptian society, and on the growing Napoleonic legend, it is held to be a failure. Costing the lives of half of the 54,000 men who participated in it, it had few practical results. The failure was caused or worsened by Napoleon's pointless over-extension into Syrian Palestine.

Revealing for the first time Napoleon's full character, both its strengths and weaknesses, the campaign was a dress rehearsal for the Russian one of 1812. Both success and failure stemmed from Napoleon's need to conquer, his inability to merely administer a peaceful society. The vast political and territorial changes caused by his great victories never lasted long. His swelling ego made him push from one victory to another, something which he did very well indeed. But if he did not leave a good peacetime administration in capable hands, the conquest seldom lasted long.

But that was not how the French people, especially the Parisians, saw things. The quick conquest of many places long associated with Christian culture, outdoing even the achievements of the French Crusades, did not harm Napoleon's reputation at all. Certainly not when contrasted with the muddled and squalid political picture at home. Whatever the grumbling Directory might think, people in the streets were only too eager to greet the conquering hero, to see him in person, and to feel better knowing he was in their midst during a time of peril. If, as a strategic maneuver against Britain, the Egyptian campaign accomplished little, as an event in Napoleon's career it was an important confirmation of the greatness implied by his successes in Italy. It became, in fact, his launching pad to supreme power. More even than on his return from Italy, Paris was like ancient Rome greeting a victorious Caesar—filled with surging, delirious crowds.

"Hail Bonaparte! Hail Bonaparte! Hail Bonaparte! . . ."

CHAPTER FOUR

First Consul

in Paris

(1799–1804)

The France to which Napoleon returned from Egypt in October 1799 was like a ship without a captain or a rudder. The people, having lived through a turbulent decade of revolution and war, were emotionally exhausted by ceaseless change. The current government functioned poorly. It consisted of a Directory and of two legislative assemblies, the Council of Ancients (something like our Senate) and the Council of Five Hundred (something like our House of Representatives). The powers of the executive were divided among five Directors, all incompetent men who were good only at talking and at intriguing against each other. Tensions were strong not only among the Directors but also between the Directory and the Councils, and, in the country at large, between monarchists and revolutionaries. In the meantime, gigantic problems went unattended: unemployment; national bankruptcy; wars going poorly against England, Russia, and Austria; monarchist rebellion in the west; radical conspiracies in Paris. No wonder the people lacked faith in their government and hope for the future.

Into this situation, therefore, Napoleon came at the right moment. As the victor in Italy and Egypt, he was very well received in France, even though he had come home from Egypt without obtaining official permission to do so. The military hero of the hour seemed to some to be the man to save the Republic, and he was approached by both Jacobin (revolutionary) leaders and Bourbon (monarchist) agents.

Napoleon, for his part, sensed that what the country needed was not this or that political party or theory of government but a single leader full of imagination and drive. By sheer coincidence, he also believed that, with his abilities, achievements, and self-confidence, he was that man. Of course, he was a soldier, not a Parisian politician. But just as he had learned military science in a very short time, so could he master the art of politics. What the professional politician had over him in experience, he himself more than made up for with genius.

Besides being a fresh new face, a young military hero, and a talent seeking a new career, Napoleon was an actor. He nicely played the role of being merely a soldier home for a vacation. He dressed in civilian clothes, went to social and cultural gatherings, and even gave a lecture to a group of appreciative scholars at the Institute of France. These were surely not the feverish actions of a man with burning ambitions, a man about to seize power.

Behind the scenes, though, he was busy. He entered into talks with several of the Directors, who, ignorant of whom or what they were dealing with, actually thought that they could make good use of him. His handle on the legislative assemblies was his younger brother Lucien, equally ambitious and cunning, who was a member of the Council of Five Hundred and even had been made, out of deference to Napoleon's presence, the president (i.e., speaker or chairman) for the month. Soon a conspiracy was knitted together.

The coup d'état, or abrupt illegal seizure of power, took place on November 9 and 10, 1799. It is often described by historians as more comedy than tragedy. Success was due to luck, to the deeds of Napoleon's associates, and to the disarray of those in the government, rather than to Napoleon's genius or actions. It went as follows. Notices of the next meeting of the two Councils were sent very late or not at all to those known to be against Napoleon. At the meeting itself, the two Councils appointed the popular Napoleon commander of all troops in Paris. As prearranged, three of the five Directors resigned, leaving the nation without an executive. At the same time, the claim was made in the Council of Five Hundred that a conspiracy against the government was afoot and therefore both legislatures should move to the safety of a suburb of Paris. The joke was that the only conspiracy afoot was the one that took the legislatures out of Paris and put them into the tender care of the soldiers supposed to protect them.

With a minimal show of force, Napoleon could easily have taken over now. But he was intent on legitimacy; he did not want to resort to naked military power. The quest for at least the appearance of legality made things move more slowly and gave his opponents time to become suspicious and alarmed. The price Napoleon had to pay for avoiding bloodshed and going through parliamentary form was that he now ran into a problem familiar to those dealing with groups of politicians: debate and inaction, as everyone tries to have a say. Napoleon's attempt to cut things short backfired. He made a speech to the Council of Ancients, in which he declared himself a defender of liberty against conspiracy; but his arrogance showed itself in his unfortunate choice of words, and one of his followers even tried to stop him from speaking any more, "General, you don't know what you are saying!"

Lucien's attempt to settle things quickly by extending an

invitation to Napoleon to appear before the Council of Five Hundred likewise boomeranged. For when the general entered the assembly hall, accompanied by a few soldiers, he found himself surrounded by hostile legislators hurling insults such as "Tyrant!" "Traitor!" "Outlaw!" Whereupon Napoleon nearly fainted and had to be pulled out by his soldiers. The great Napoleon—the general who had stood calmly in the midst of battle while shells burst all about him and soldiers panicked —was unnerved by a group of civilians, some quite old, bombarding him with mere words.

What saved him was his brother's quick mind. Faced with a motion to declare Napoleon an outlaw, Lucien rushed to some nearby soldiers and, talking wildly of a British-led conspiracy, got them to chase out the politicians. Their gowns flying, the councillors rushed through doors and windows.

Rounding up whatever sympathetic members of the Council of Five Hundred he could find, Lucien had them vote for acceptance of the resignation of the five Directors and the temporary appointment of three consuls. (A consul was the man in charge of the executive for one year at a time in republican, preimperial Rome, a period that was a favorite role model for revolutionary France.) One of the three consuls was Napoleon.

Then, in what is in effect a coup within the coup, Napoleon eclipsed the other two consuls in a matter of days and took sole control of the reins of power. He adapted a proposed new constitution to his own needs and had himself made First Consul for ten years, with full governing power.

What with the incompetence of the Directory and the superstar quality of Napoleon, Paris took the change of government in its stride. The rapidity and bloodlessness of the event also made it seem a good thing or, at worst, insignificant. People little realized what a gigantic alteration had actually taken place. Exciting and turbulent as the previous ten years had been—a decade filled with a rapid turnover in leaders, governments, and even forms of government—they were now to be followed, under the unbroken leadership of one man, by fifteen years of equal excitement, achievement, and disaster. The French Revolution, which had brought to the fore so many outstanding individuals who might otherwise have remained obscure—Lafayette, Mirabeau, Marat, Danton, Carnot, Robespierre—in its dying gasp gave political birth to by far the greatest, or at any rate the most enduring and consequential, of them all.

A month and a half later, on December 25, 1799, the new constitution went into operation, and Napoleon, as First Consul, was more powerful than the kings recently overthrown. In February, he even transferred his residence to the Tuileries, the official Paris residence of the kings. In a national vote held at that time, over three million voters said "yes" and only some fifteen hundred said "no" to the new constitution and the new ruler. Could any king anywhere have ever shown such popularity?

Napoleon wasted no time in establishing himself. There were immediate critical matters to be attended to, and there were those chronic deep-seated problems. Most of us operate on the principle of "one at a time," "haste makes waste," and "as soon as possible." But a political genius like Napoleon operated on the principle of "everything at once" and "sooner than possible." He got a lot done that way, and the historian, with his need to analyze and clarify, is forced to separate in his narrative what Napoleon, like a juggler or magician, handled at the same time.

First, Napoleon had to set up a new form of government, a new political system, in fact. What he wanted—and quickly received—was a constitution that provided for a First Consul with broad powers who towered over various legislative bodies with limited powers. There was a Tribunate to debate but not vote and a Legislature to vote but not debate. The First Consul surrounded himself with a Council of State consisting of the best men he could find regardless of their politics, family, or

*Napoleon before the Council of Five Hundred, 10 November 1799, being
called a traitor and an outlaw. He then fainted, but the coup d'etat
succeeded anyway.*

party. Under the strict control of Napoleon, this council drew up the laws, applied them, and even passed legal judgment on them. To make sure that his will was the only one that mattered, Napoleon had the councillors consult with him individually. To meet with all of them together as part of cabinet sessions would be to set up a possible rival power bloc. As the Romans had said, "Divide and Conquer."

Napoleon's new powers had to be used promptly to establish long-needed law and order. Using the army effectively, Napoleon quickly pacified the western area of France by snuffing out the ongoing monarchist rebellion there. Concurrently, he harassed the extremists on the other end of the political spectrum, the Jacobins or radicals, who were always trying to form conspiracies. He also cleared the roads of bands of highwaymen who were crippling commerce and agriculture. At the same time, while cracking down on political extremists of every stripe, he invited back all exiles, both those of the old monarchic regime driven out by the Revolution and those revolutionaries and radicals driven out by recent governments. He welcomed all who were willing to compromise their principles in order to work with each other and with him for the good of France— but always as that good was defined by him. For he saw or presented himself as above party, a self-made man, the prisoner of no class or special interest, the choice of all the people (unlike the traditional ruler who gets his power by inherited privilege), and the unifier of a nation long divided by and into monarchists and revolutionaries. He was far more interested in practical ideas and efficiency, in intelligence and energy, than in theories and slogans.

This was in fact a secret of Napoleon's early success at home, his achievements and popularity, his greatness as a politician. He had a unique ability to take good ideas wherever he found them. He also had the rare sense to ignore the bad ideas to which the good ones were attached when they were, as is often the case, parts of systems, philosophies, party platforms.

This knack enabled him to combine the best in the old monarchical system with the best in the new revolutionary principles.

The old Bourbon monarchy was a dead thing in France as far as he could see; he even told a claimant to the throne to forget about a restoration of the monarchy because it would cost a hundred thousand lives. Yet the idea of one-man rule, of concentrated power, is not bad when the man in charge has the right dynamism. And since he knew of someone who would make a good one-man ruler—himself—he set up such a form of government, although (at least at first) without any of the trappings of the disgraced monarchy. The language and the forms of government were republican, revolutionary.

On the other hand, he appreciated the achievements of the Revolution. Its battle cry of "Liberty, Equality, Fraternity," he translated into his own slogan of "careers open to talent" without distinctions of birth. The Revolution was based on the principle that great men can appear in any social class or condition of life, and it had pumped new vitality into the nation by using such men to replace a privileged class that had long ceased to consist of the best. Was not Napoleon's own career a supreme example of that principle? The people he hired to head the various agencies of government were the best available and therefore gave France the best administration in its history.

To encourage and reward talent, Napoleon established (in 1802) a Legion of Honor. As a replacement for the abolished and unjustly privileged aristocracy, the Legion would honor men of any background who had made great strides in any field of human endeavor. The honor was not hereditary: the great man's children could not get into the Legion unless they made it by their own achievements. This was a democratic, revolutionary, egalitarian notion of aristocracy.

One might ask, Why have such a Legion at all, when talent, like virtue, is (or should be) its own reward? Because, said Napoleon with brutal candor, people want toys; men love honor and need distinctions. Such a view may be cynical about human nature, but appears to have made for shrewd psychology and politics. The idea of the Legion of Honor was ridiculed, but Napoleon imposed it, and it has survived to this day as one of the great institutions of France.

The belief that people need toys also shaped Napoleon's approach to another important governmental question, religion. The old monarchy had been married to the Catholic Church; the Revolution had divorced church and state. On the question of whether religion is "true" and whether God exists, Napoleon had no deep feelings; he thought it unanswerable and in any case not relevant to his interests. At issue were not his personal opinions but what the people wanted. Religion as generally practiced seemed to Napoleon to be one of the "toys" that people needed. Therefore, he set about making, after long and difficult negotiations with Rome, a settlement with the Vatican.

According to this Concordat of 1801–2, the Catholic Church was made again, in effect, the established church of France and of its rulers. But the Church had to accommodate itself to some of the principles of the Revolution (and the needs of Napoleonic dictatorship). That is, other religions were tolerated from now on; church lands distributed to the peasants could be kept by them; and the French government, the secular authority—i.e. Napoleon—retained veto power over Church appointments, actions, and publications within France.

To both those favoring the Revolution and to the adherents of the old regime, the Concordat was a sell-out by Napoleon and by the pope. Yet Napoleon believed, probably correctly, that such a lightly established Church was what the mass of the French people wanted, because they were still deeply Catholic, at least in a cultural if not in a religious way. Politically, the Concordat also had the merit of driving the Church and the French clergy away from France's enemies and reconciling them with the French state.

Napoleon as First Consul (early 1800s).

In making himself a mere consul, setting up a Legion of Honor, and reestablishing in a way the Catholic Church, Napoleon altered those old but disgraced institutions—the monarchy, aristocracy, and church—by modernizing them, making them fit a more revolutionary, democratic age. He was, in short, a moderate, a great compromiser and pragmatist, someone favoring evolution over both revolution and the status quo, someone who takes the middle of the road, who tries for what is workable rather than true, or perfect, or ideal. Politics, it has been said, is the art of the possible; and Napoleon when young knew more about the possible than almost anyone. That is another secret of his political greatness.

Besides settling these broad institutional questions and reconciling the monarchical past with the revolutionary present, Napoleon quickly put his mind to numerous current practical issues. To help solve unemployment, he had men work for the state. The national treasury was nearly bankrupt when he took over, and he met that challenge by coercing the bankers into forming a national Bank of France so that the government no longer had to borrow money from private individuals. He established a vast modern educational system, including a University of France, open to people of all ranks. Among his many other accomplishments in these first years were a revitalization of the tax-collecting system, stimulation of manufacturing and science, the energizing and regulation of the financial markets, the stabilization of the currency, a crackdown on fraud and on profiteering among those doing business with the army and on speculators in the currency.

He modernized and streamlined the administration of the country. The nation was divided into about a hundred departments, each headed by a prefect. The First Consul or his Council of State appointed the prefects, who in turn appointed local officials and monitored their work at the county and town level. This centralized government was more efficient than anything under even the powerful King Louis XIV. It is basically still in place today.

To administer the nation a set of laws was needed. The French legal system had long been acknowledged by everyone to be a mess, a self-contradictory hodgepodge of written laws and customs, of national and local laws, of feudal and revolutionary laws. Recent governments of both sides had begun the vast task of reforming and simplifying the system but had not gotten far. The first act of Napoleon's reign was to start the process that resulted in one of his greatest achievements, a unified legal system. Napoleon put together the best French legal minds, regardless of their philosophies, and gave them a deadline. Making them work late into the night, often joining in their deliberations, asking perceptive questions, and applying to every law the twin tests of "justice" and "usefulness" in contemporary society, he got them to hammer out in a brief period a short, compact book that is one of the glories of Western civilization. This Civil Code, made part of the French constitution in 1804, came to be known as the Napoleonic Code. It is the basis today of legal systems in many parts of the world (including the state of Louisiana). It incorporates many of the central modern "liberal" ideas of the Revolution: abolishing a hereditary nobility, confirming the breaking up of the large estates held by aristocracy and Church, establishing civil and religious rights, civil marriage and divorce, children's rights. To modern eyes, however, it perhaps gives men too much power over women, fathers over children, property owners over the propertyless, the state over the individual. Again we see the taking of the middle ground between radicalism and do-nothing conservatism.

These are only some of the accomplishments of the new government under Napoleon. All France, especially Paris, reveled in the new efficiency and prosperity, the new peace and stability. Nothing like it had been seen in the last century of the declining monarchy or in the years of the Revolution. In two busy and creative years, the first of his fifteen-year reign, Napoleon established, or began, a restructuring of French society that is even more important and remarkable than his military and diplomatic achievements and that is considered the greatest progressive change in the history of Europe. The creation of a modern nation-state, in England or America the work of many men through many decades, had been carried out by the vision and determination of one Frenchman in a matter of months. He may have had the ground prepared for him by the revolutionary decade; he may have been a dictator and a war lover, but Napoleon, at least in his early years, more than any similarly placed and similarly inclined individual in history—Caesar, Cromwell, Louis XIV—probably contributed more to civilization than he took from it.

No wonder that a thriving, prosperous France felt confident of itself and proud of Napoleon. Well might they accept the rather presumptuous sentence in the proclamation made soon after the 1799 coup d'état: "Citizens, the revolution has returned to the principles with which it began. It is at an end." The word *end* is nicely double-edged. It can mean "finished, broken, stopped, undone, aborted" or it can mean "fulfilled, brought to fruition, realized." In Napoleon's hands, it came to mean both.

For it must be admitted that all these dazzling accomplishments went hand in hand with a swollen ego and a boundless ambition for the highest powers and fame. When in retirement, he looked over his achievements and said, "In this gigantic struggle between the [revolutionary, progressive] present and the [monarchical, tradition-oriented] past, I am the natural arbiter and mediator. I tried to be its supreme judge. My whole internal administration, my whole foreign policy were determined by that great aim." *He* had saved the Revolution, which he claimed was dying. *He* had washed off its crimes and held up the noble core for Europe to emulate. *He* had planted new ideas in Europe that time could not alter.

These words express both the truth of his achievement and the vanity of one who thought he was irreplaceable and who glossed over the rivers of blood shed in the course of that achievement. Modesty was never a trait of his. Of his seizing power, he said that the nation sought out the one man who could save it, the man who could not do so until he was known, and knew himself, to be "a guardian angel." He had a responsibility, a patriotic duty, to replace the incompetent Directory by extralegal means. He saw himself, as he saw Julius Caesar, to be expressing the popular will and therefore in the deepest sense legitimate.

Only time would tell how the struggle in his soul between the creative, beneficient statesman and the selfish, heartless adventurer would come out. For the moment, the statesman seemed to be stronger, but was not the adventurer growing? Was there not already in him the presumptuous attitude that he would put into words years later when he said, "France needs me more than I need France"?

Napoleon understood very well the leading question posterity would ask about him: "People will wonder whether or not I really aimed at universal monarchy . . . whether my immense ambition was spurred by lust for power or glory or love of general welfare." Then he slammed the door and left us with the mystery: "I often would have found it very difficult to assert what was my whole and real intention." When, as consul, he was asked where he was heading, "I always answered that I had not the least idea." The answer astonished everyone.

CHAPTER FIVE

Emperor
of the French
(1800–1805)

W hile busy with these enormous administrative, social, and legal reforms, Napoleon also kept his
keen eyes on foreign affairs. It is almost impossible
to believe that the four years of the Consulate, during which
the rebellions in western France were put down, the Church
was reestablished, the Civil Code, the Legion of Honor, the
civil service systems, and the University of France were begun,
and which saw the rise of the nation from a decade of chaos to
unrivaled prosperity, was also a period of military conquest and
diplomatic achievement, of great strides in the extension of
French domination in Europe.

In December 1799, Napoleon broke with tradition by
sending letters directly to the king of England and the Austrian
emperor, instead of, as was the norm, to their ministers. The
letters sounded like peace feelers, but even as he sent them, he

was urging his troops to be ready to invade rather than merely defend. When the letters went unanswered, as he no doubt expected them to be, he felt free to turn to war. Peace might be the end, but war was the means.

The first problem facing him was that the Italy he had so nicely conquered in 1796–97 had fallen out of French control. After resupplying the French army there and putting it on a better war footing, Napoleon crossed the Alps on a mule and took personal command of the forces. (He thus violated the current law against consuls exercising military field command.) His immediate task was to relieve a French force besieged in Genoa and to liberate the province of Lombardy.

Napoleon led the army into battle against a large Austrian force at Marengo in June 1800. For once, he committed various errors in strategy, such as splitting up his main force (something he often warned his generals against). An Austrian attack caught him by surprise. He lost his bearings and had to let his subordinate commanders improvise. At another point, the French were thrown back in confusion, and the battle appeared lost. A nervous Napoleon barely stopped his troops from panicking by telling them that reserves were on the way.

Perhaps worry over what might happen politically in Paris during his absence threw his timing and intuition off. The frequent remarks in his letters to his political colleagues that he would soon be back in Paris suggest the new First Consul's insecurity over what was going on behind his back in the capital and over not having strong support there to fall back on if he lost a battle. He was free of such anxieties in the campaigns of 1796–97, when he was only a general and not a politician back home as well. Something of that insecurity remained with him throughout his career and helps to explain his need to pile up victories endlessly.

Good luck, however, together with a host of errors by the Austrians, enabled him to turn defeat into a splendid victory. So splendid, in fact, that once again Austria lost control of most of northern Italy. At home, the victory at Marengo had a powerful impact too. It became a byword for military brilliance. It consolidated his power and set back his political enemies, who had hoped for his defeat in battle. How daring for the head of a new government to risk everything on the battlefield! Hope of restoring the pretender Louis XVIII to the French throne began to fade, and men who looked to a monarchy started to think of making Napoleon king rather than having a Bourbon ruler restored.

Napoleon urged the Austrians to make peace. When he got no clear response, he sent his armies into action again. Soon enough, the Austrians saw the light and signed the Treaty of Lunéville, which was a replay or confirmation of the earlier treaty. Meanwhile, he annexed the Piedmont and renamed the recently established Cisalpine Republic the Italian Republic, with himself as president. He ended a civil war in nearby Switzerland and stopped British intrigues there. The federal constitution he imposed on the Swiss made him one of the fathers of modern Switzerland. He turned the country into a satellite of France.

The Treaty of Lunéville was soon followed by the Treaty of Amiens negotiated with the British. After ten years of war ushered in by the French Revolution, there was immense gratitude for the military hero who had made a glorious peace. This "Peace of the Consulate" was to be rewarded (despite some dissent) with the grant of the consulship for life. Napoleon seemed to have reached what for lesser mortals would be the fulfillment of a career.

Historians play the difficult game of pinpointing which year saw the true zenith of a life filled with an unbelievable number of high points. Suggestions range from 1802 to 1812. Those who pick 1802 point to the Concordat with the pope, the Treaty of Amiens, and the consulship for life as a series of climaxes to the French Revolution, the war in Europe, and Napoleon's rise to power. This was the year when Napoleon proved himself to be a statesman, a peace-making politician with his own mind and will, and without yet showing the malevolent, dictatorial, warmongering side of his character. From March 1802 to April 1803, France was at peace, the Consulate at its finest, and the country lived in a Golden Age. Even poor Louis XVIII had addressed Napoleon as "the victor of Lodi, Castiglione, and Arcole, the Conqueror of Italy and Egypt" and the "savior of France."

On Easter Sunday in April 1802, a week after the publication of the Concordat and a day after the ratification of the Treaty of Amiens, Napoleon participated in a High Mass and *Te Deum* at Notre Dame cathedral. All the government officials and prominent Parisians turned out for this celebration of peace in Europe and of reconciliation with the Church at home. Thousands of people crowded the streets to watch the procession to the church. Inside, a massive choir sang the venerable Latin words as the fragrance of the incense, the colors of the vestments, and the solemn intonations of the priests assaulted the senses of those fortunate enough to have gained entry. Officially, this was a rendering of thanks to the Creator—"Glory to God in the Highest"—but in reality it was an almost sacrilegious celebration of one man's rise. In his privileged seat up front, Napoleon might well have felt that he had achieved—at age thirty-two and in only five years—a success given to few individuals in history.

Napoleon early on established the royal palace of the Tuileries as his official residence, a symbol of his ambitions. As First Consul, he quickly monopolized all power. He eclipsed the other two consuls, who were nominally his equals, and the various legislative and judicial assemblies with which he was supposed to share responsibility. He made all the appointments to top legislative, judicial, executive, and civil service posts. Then in August 1802, in the euphoria over his recent achievements, he had himself made First Consul for life, with the right to choose his successor. On encountering opposition in the Tribunate, he ordered a referendum on the matter. He won that by a vote of three and a half million to eight thousand. (Although a tribute to his undoubted popularity, the results of all the Napoleonic referenda remind us that he invented the modern dictator's technique of rigging elections for the sake of public relations, for the appearance of democracy and unanimity.) Then he proposed yet another constitution, one to fit the needs of a supreme First Consul for life, and further subordinated the legislatures.

Two years later, in the spring of 1804, against the background of the beginnings of the Third Coalition of nations against post-Revolutionary France, Napoleon had himself proclaimed, in violation of the current constitution, hereditary Emperor of the French. The justification for making the empire hereditary was that potential assassins would be deterred by the knowledge that killing Napoleon would merely bring in another Bonaparte.

This action was more a change in labels than a real change in government. It solved the problem of succession, appeased those republicans fearful of a return of the Bourbon kings, and gave the royalists a substitute monarchy, which prevented a civil war or a resumption of chaos and anarchy. And so a hereditary autocracy, the very thing the Revolution had been against, was created.

Napoleon had a theory to justify his somewhat shocking action. He believed that the Revolutionary slogan, "Liberty, Equality, Fraternity," was in good part nonsense. A few intellectuals want "Liberty," but most people want glory rather than freedom, equality under a strong leader rather than liberty in a noisy democracy. They do not mind being enslaved to a heroic leader as long as they know that everyone is equally subjected, that no one is exempt or privileged. Or, to put it differently, by "equality" they do not mean a leveling down but an equality of opportunity to become superior. "Equality in the sense that everyone will be master—there you have the secret. What must be done, then, is to give everybody the hope of being able to rise." He would give them what they wanted and reserve all the rest for himself. The French would not complain; and, indeed, for a long time they did not.

To be sure, there was much to be said on all sides of the political spectrum against someone becoming king after the recent overthrow of a monarchy—especially when that person was a commoner (and formerly not even a Frenchman, at that) and when he now presumed to be not just a king but an emperor, something France had not had for a thousand years. And many intellectuals, who had been following Napoleon's quick rise with admiration and awe, washed their hands of him and turned away in disillusionment.

A typical though dramatic case was that of the German, Beethoven, perhaps the greatest composer of all time. This genius had been working on one of his masterpieces, the Third Symphony, which helped usher in nineteenth-century Romantic music. In the main room of his humble living quarters in Vienna, the score lay on a table, with a title page which had on the top in large letters, "BONAPARTE," and at the bottom "Luigi van Beethoven." The heroism of the French liberator was to be echoed and expressed by heaven-storming music.

One day, a musician friend came to tell Beethoven that Napoleon was having himself proclaimed emperor. Beethoven's strikingly dramatic face, with its stark features and wild hair, grew suddenly tense with shock and rage. He abruptly went over to the table and, with a snarl, tore off the title page, ripped it to shreds, and flung them to the ground. "Then he, too, is nothing but an ordinary mortal!" he bellowed. "Now he also will raise himself up above all others and become a tyrant!"

In Britain, another country which like Austria suffered much at the hands of Napoleon, the great Romantic poet Lord Byron likewise had a change of heart and lamented in several poems that a man who was "a single step" away from Washington's greatness could so decline. Byron contrasted the now self-centered Napoleon with the patriotic, noble Washington. Napoleon himself was aware that people were drawing such a parallel at his expense, and, never at a loss for words, he had an answer. His point was that he, like all men, was a child of circumstances. If he had been in America, he would have become a Washington, and, if Washington had lived in France, he would have had to act like Napoleon or go under like a fool. Napoleon claimed to be most eager to exhibit Washington's "moderation, disinterestedness, and wisdom," but—France being what she was and Europe being what it was and both being unlike America—he could only do it as a "crowned Washington" and "by means of a world dictatorship."

A third sensitive person alienated by what Napoleon was doing was the Marquis de Lafayette, a prominent figure in both the American and the early stages of the French Revolution. Napoleon was contemptuous of Lafayette's mind: a man who thought that the French are like the Americans and that British ideas and experiences could be applied to France had, Napoleon asserted, nothing to teach anyone about running France.

But intellectuals do not run countries, and Napoleon knew better than they did what the French people wanted and needed. A referendum ratified his becoming emperor by an official tally of 3,370,000 to 2,567 or better than 1,000 to 1. However rigged the election figures might have been, it was and is clear that the bulk of the French people approved of the elevation of their hero and that all Frenchmen, regardless of their political views, desperately depended on his military and diplomatic genius to see them through the growing military threat from abroad. That need silenced nearly all dissent. Napoleon had chosen his time deliberately, carefully.

Napoleon was not only needed; he was also very popular. He had financed his wars by taxing the conquered, not the French, people; as he said, the French armies "must feed themselves on war at the expense of enemy territory." Large sums given his generals were meant to popularize the Empire with the military. Thanks to a very well-run treasury and to the loot brought back from the defeated countries, France was free of national debt. The country prospered. Agriculture, industry, and commerce made great strides.

Above all, Napoleon as emperor greatly increased the amount and scope of construction work begun in the Consulate. Besides providing many jobs and helping commerce, it was a visible sign of order and grandeur. Many harbors were renovated. Numerous wide roads, canals, bridges were built. Swamps were drained, churches and palaces restored, factories set up for the unemployed, banks and museums opened or vastly enlarged, cities beautified, horse racing and sheep breeding instituted. Paris especially was beautified, as it was to be the "true" ecclesiastical and political "capital of Europe," something "fabulous, colossal, unprecedented," and the center of all the arts and archives of civilization. "I want to force every king in Europe to build a large palace for his use in Paris. When an Emperor of the French is crowned, these kings shall come to Paris." His treasures, Napoleon boasted, were not gold and money hoards, rumored to be in the basement of the Tuileries palace, but "immense and in the open for everyone to see," and they would "endure for centuries." If the British Empire was held together by common interests, the French one was held together by the will and the splendid deeds of one popular man.

And, in the background, by the power of arms. For, in case popularity and construction work were not enough, Napoleon believed that a little coercion and repression could not hurt the state. More and more his regime took on the repressiveness of the overthrown Bourbon kings. Actually, because of typical Napoleonic efficiency, it was more repressive. The kings of the past had been restrained by tradition, custom, church, aristocracy. Now nothing stood between the ruler's will and the people. The old institutions, however unjust or irrational, had something to be said for them after all, but the work of modernization had been done all too well by the French Revolution—and by Napoleon. Sometimes one cannot be sure whether the Napoleonic regime was the last benevolent, enlightened despotism or the first modern totalitarian state.

The ten years of the Empire were not as filled with domestic reforms as the four of the Consulate, partly because Napoleon was busy with foreign policy and war-making and mainly because of the growing conservation of his dictatorship. The great liberal reforms of the Consulate were being matched by the reactionary measures of the Empire.

Political bodies were tampered with so as to eliminate all freedom. The arts, especially the theater, were subjected to censorship. The number of newspapers and journals allowed to publish was severely reduced, and the remainder were supervised and censored. Books were burned, and even school assemblies and private correspondence monitored. A powerful secret police and espionage system was established, with agents and spies everywhere—or at least thought to be everywhere. Various new legal documents followed the laws of the Bourbon monarchy. To education and to teachers was brought a military and almost monastic discipline, as the minister of education in Paris controlled every aspect of the learning process anywhere in the realm. Higher education was encouraged but watered down, with free inquiry less emphasized than the justification of the social system created by Napoleon and of his version of morality and politics.

Religious training was encouraged, notably for women, who had to learn that their place in life consisted of producing and raising citizen-soldiers for the state. Religion had high priority, not because Napoleon was a believer but because he politically, or cynically, thought of it as necessary for keeping people in line and making them obedient to the state. He therefore used the Concordat for his own purpose, as he did even the Church's catechism: additions to it taught pupils that submission to the Emperor Napoleon was enjoined by St. Paul! He even had a St. Napoleon's Day celebration (after an obscure saint by that name) added to the calendar. Nothing was beyond his reach; at home now as much as he had been in the past in the battle for Italy, Napoleon was a modern master of insinuation and propaganda, of what would now be called the "cult of personality."

He could also be ruthless when necessary. A bomb plot in late 1800 became the convenient occasion for executing or exiling over a hundred radicals. Various other opposition figures were driven from Paris. Perhaps most shocking to contemporary Europe was the Duke d'Enghien case. The kidnapping of a prince of the royal blood and his execution in March 1804 after a mock trial hurt Napoleon's reputation as a hero-statesman. Perhaps he thought that by shedding Bourbon blood he bolstered his credentials as a revolutionary. Many observers agreed with one of his own ministers who made the famous remark that this killing was "worse than a crime; it was a blunder."

The inauguration of the Empire merely speeded up tendencies already present before. Assemblies became rubber stamp organizations to ratify his ordinances. The Revolutionary, Republican title of "citizen" applied to everyone was replaced by the more traditional "monsieur" (which originally meant "my sire," "my lord"). Generals became, as under the Bourbon kings, "marshals." Napoleon amply rewarded those who helped him rise to power, some with large incomes, mansions, and estates. He established a whole new aristocracy with hereditary estates and with titles (prince, duke, count, baron, knight) fashioned on those in traditional monarchies. The titles would impress everyone, dilute the old nobility, and create loyalty. The aristocracy, which had been the growth of centuries with a power base independent of the king, was now, with one stroke by Napoleon, created anew overnight and was utterly dependent on him.

No one ever had done such a thing before, certainly not in modern times. Napoleon's half-convincing official justification was the need to reconcile France with Europe, old France with new France, and to associate nobility with service to the state rather than with arbitrary feudal privilege. But if service by the individual was the criterion, how could the honor be hereditary? And if Napoleon wanted to make his generals more loyal and efficient by freeing them of money worries, his generosity had the reverse result of making them want to enjoy their prosperity in leisure rather than continue fighting all their lives.

He began placing his brothers, as well as his other relatives and his generals, on various subsidiary royal and ducal thrones (in Holland, Naples, Spain, and lesser places). He married them off into royal families, without, of course, consulting their personal preferences. His generals, often coming from a low social class, were encouraged to marry into the traditional aristocracies of Europe as a way of spreading his Empire, cementing the loyalty of his followers, and reconciling old families with new achievers. From everyone whom he rewarded, the price exacted was the same: obedience and submission. Whatever their title, they were still French princes, subject to the whims of the emperor.

As a framework or nerve center, an imperial court with a regular etiquette was established. Decrees setting up many complex new titles and settling complicated questions of precedence were issued. Napoleon also commissioned works of art and offered prizes for outstanding artists as part of the celebration of the new imperial grandeur.

Becoming emperor was not enough. To gain legitimacy and to awe the world, Napoleon wanted to be crowned by the pope, as were the Austrian emperors. And, true to his character, he would go them one better by having the pope come to Paris to perform the ceremony—as if the pontiff were Napoleon's private chaplain. The reluctant Holy Father finally yielded to

In this sketch, Napoleon, his back rudely turned to the Pope, crowns himself Emperor of the French, in Notre Dame Cathedral, 2 December 1804.

Napoleon's magnetism, or power, though not before forcing Napoleon's civil marriage to Josephine to be solemnized in a church ceremony.

During a grand spectacle in Notre Dame cathedral on December 2, 1804, Napoleon, after being anointed by the pope, took the crown from him and placed it on his own head and then crowned Josephine as empress. In another typical touch

*This is a detail of a canvas by the most famous French painter of the day,
J.L. David, who shows Napoleon's mother (in a special seat) smiling
over the scene—even though she was not actually present at
the coronation.*

of personal vanity, he had insisted beforehand that he would not have the crown placed on his head by the pope lest that symbolize some sort of Churchly superiority. Nor would he, as part of the ceremony, swear to be dependent on the pope. He even refused to participate in the Mass celebrated on that occasion.

He modeled the ceremony, as he now did his career, on Charlemagne, the great medieval French ruler, who had founded the Holy Roman Empire and who had been crowned at Rome a thousand years earlier as "Emperor of the Romans." Even the design of the crown was a replica of Charlemagne's. Napoleon acted as though he were in the direct succession from Charlemagne and the Roman emperors. "I am Charlemagne, for like Charlemagne I have united the crowns of France and Lombardy, and my Empire extends to the borders of the Orient . . . I am Charlemagne, the sword of the Church and the clergy's Emperor." He was thereby challenging the Hapsburg rulers of Austria, who claimed to be descended from Charlemagne and for four centuries had been called the Holy Roman Emperors.

Since he had also been president of the Italian Republic, he now called himself King of Italy. He had himself crowned in an even more impressive ceremony in Milan (May 1805) and then went on a triumphal procession through jubilant Italian cities. The two coronations surely rank as another climax in his career, on a par with the Easter *Te Deum* marking the achievements and euphoria of 1802.

At the coronation at Milan the iron crown of Lombardy, formerly the symbol of Austrian supremacy in Italy, was placed on his head. He was going out of his way to snub Austria, the leading power in central Europe. This showed ambitions far beyond the "natural" frontiers of France. It led directly to the formation of the Third Coalition against France.

Napoleon often decried war but distinguished between a whimsical war, which he called a "criminal" act, and a war justified by the policy of one's nation. His own wars were caused by a good policy, the desire for peace—but (and here comes a gigantic cop-out) a "glorious" peace rather than just any peace, a "solemn, durable" peace, and a peace that meets the needs of France.

Those adjectives provide a loophole large enough to drive a conquering army through and to allow it to bring back on its return trip an empire as vast as man can dream.

CHAPTER SIX

The First
Napoleonic War
(1802–1807)

When Napoleon in early 1802 signed the Treaty of Amiens with Britain, people in both countries were ecstatic. Although the terms were rather favorable to France, many believed that an era of peace had begun. It turned out instead to be only a truce in the long struggle between the great land power of France and the great sea power of Britain for the mastery of Europe. During the peaceful interlude, the British reneged on their promise to evacuate Egypt and Malta (both of which they had taken from the French after Napoleon had left the army there and gone on to bigger feats). For his part, Napoleon made various moves that violated the spirit if not the letter of the treaty. His hints that Egypt could easily be reconquered particularly aroused British indignation. Both sides were on a collision course.

This marks a watershed in Napoleon's career, when the attractive traits that marked his rapid ascendancy to power, began to be overshadowed by the unattractive traits brought out by the corruptions of power. Having achieved personal primacy in France and national primacy for France, he, as most men in his place would have done, could have rested on his laurels and governed a harmonious, prosperous people in a peaceful continent. But Napoleon, as he had already shown in Egypt, was too restless ever to do that. He always had to find new worlds to annex. Unable to treat other nations as allies or equals of France, he was an empire builder. Because of his temperament and philosophy, Napoleon as emperor was developing a momentum that would lead from one war to another—with the appropriate name of the Napoleonic Wars. His philosophy, which was in part a rationalization for, or dressing up of, his naked lust for power, was that a government based on revolution (unlike one based on a traditional monarchy) could only stand on the crisis of war and the glitter of conquest. If it abandoned that, it would fall.

Therefore peace turned into a cold war with Britain. The British were certainly no angels, but Napoleon's actions never gave them the chance to be. They had long been committed to a policy of a balance of powers, according to which no one nation on the continent was to have the ability to dictate terms to the rest. They therefore could not tolerate French domination of Europe. Napoleon understood this position and acted accordingly. Although he did not expect a break with Britain before 1805, both sides were busily preparing for a resumption of hostilities. It came sooner than expected, in May 1803.

The campaigns Napoleon had been involved in until now were part of the long war of 1792–1802 created by the confrontation of Revolutionary France with the traditional monarchies. The idea of spreading revolutionary principles by war, achieving French domination over old European monarchies, and surrounding France with sympathetic, modernized nations had actually been given to Napoleon by France's earlier Revolutionary governments, which saw France as a beacon to Europe. That war had not been of his making, but it enabled him to find himself, his vocation, his greatness.

For this war of 1803–1815, however, Napoleon must be held responsible. From about 1796 to 1802, the destiny of France and of Napoleon met and merged. What was good for the one was good for the other. From 1803 on, they diverged, and France was forced beyond her natural frontiers into adventures that were neither French nor Revolutionary but Napoleonic. The Grand Empire, as it came to be called, was more of a personal than a national aspiration—although the French people, seduced by Napoleon's magnificent victories and acquisitions, took a long time to become aware of it.

With the coming of war, Napoleon, ever the man to look for a quick knock-out blow (what we could call a "blitzkrieg" or lightning war), went back to his ideas of 1797 for an invasion of Britain. He first planned a night crossing of the Channel during the winter of 1803–4. Then he made a timetable for the late summer of 1804. When that did not materialize, it was set for June 1805. Such plans were helped along by Spain's entry into the war on the French side. But even when he had collected a thousand troop-carrying flat-bottomed boats by the end of 1804, he realized that that was not enough. In the spring of 1805, he developed a concrete plan based on the operations of three large French-Spanish fleets.

The problem he grappled with was British naval supremacy. His answer to the problem was a planned diversion to the Caribbean, which would draw off the mass of the British war fleet, or at least that dangerous man Nelson. While the British were on a wild-goose chase, the flat-bottomed boats would make the short channel crossing to Britain and land a hundred thousand men. This army, executing a quick march to London, would decapitate Britain in four days. With a newly established

British republic replacing the monarchy and aristocracy and with the British populace currently the worst treated "in the world," Napoleon would be received in Britain, as in Italy and Egypt, as a liberator, not a conqueror. And with the British monarchy overthrown, "Europe will be at our feet."

The fallacy in this ambitious scenario was Napoleon's assumption that the British, like the French, were more interested in a particular form of government—say, a republican democracy—than in a traditional way of life, British society with all its illogic and unfairness. He assumed that the average British shopkeeper, worker, or farmer would show greater fondness for Frenchmen bearing liberal principles than for fellow Britons who happened to be dukes and industrialists. Reason would certainly dictate such a preference, and Napoleon was a child of the Age of Reason—but the British, in the main, were not.

Wonderful and easy as all this seemed, Napoleon was sensible enough to realize that as long as the French admirals lacked the initiative of his generals the time was not yet ripe. The admirals, in fact, nearly drove him up a wall. In session after session, he would propose a plan of action only to have "the whole navy on my neck":

"Sire, this is impossible."

"Why?"

"Sire, the winds don't allow it, and then the doldrums, the currents. . . ."

With that, they brought each plan to an abrupt end. Napoleon would take no such nonsense from his generals because he knew the military art and the military jargon ten times better than they did, but with the navy he was out of his element. Many a time he brought his fist down on his desk or nervously slapped his riding crop against his thigh and cried out, half to himself, half to everyone within hearing: "How can a man argue with people who speak a different language?" Many a time he paced nervously in his office and complained that all naval undertakings in his regime have "invariably failed because the admirals have picked up the notion, I know not where, that one can make war without taking any risks." Many a time he looked at his handsome warships wasting uselessly in the harbor and muttered to himself the wish that he had a Nelson under his command. "Things would have taken a different turn. . . ." And then he had to shift his thoughts from dreams of brilliant naval victories back to things as they unfortunately were.

Finally, he came to see that new challenges in Central Europe would have to be dealt with before he could have a showdown with Britain. Turning the Italian Republic into a hereditary kingdom—with himself crowned as king, of course —had created much hostility in Europe and had led to the formation of a new alliance against him. What drove the nail into the coffin of Napoleon's planned invasion of Britain at this time, and indeed of all French naval warfare, was Nelson's great victory at Trafalgar against a powerful French-Spanish fleet off the Spanish coast in October 1805.

Just as he had in 1797 given up the invasion of Britain as impractical for the moment and turned instead to Egypt, so did he, eight years later, again shift from Britain to the East. In August 1805, he rapidly focused his attention on Central Europe. He rushed his Grand Army—as the gathering of forces for the invasion of Britain had come to be known—to the Danube. There, the Austrians, together with the Russians, were massing for a campaign.

The Austrian Emperor Francis, we saw, was particularly offended by Napoleon's consolidation of his hold on Italy and his theft of the title to the Holy Roman Empire, the succession to Charlemagne claimed by the Austrians. So, Francis made common cause with the new czar of Russia, Alexander I, who was as concerned as other Europeans were with keeping France within bounds. Reversing his father's pro-French policy, the czar had signed a treaty with Britain directed against France (April 1805). Reluctantly Austria joined the new alliance to form the Third Coalition. The continental powers would put armies in the field, while Britain would patrol the seas and help foot the bill. Napoleon decided to take care of Austria first, then Russia, then Britain. He planned to seize Vienna and quickly abort the new coalition. He therefore gave Austria an ultimatum—to withdraw from the Tyrol and to remain neutral —which he knew she would turn down.

The Austrians were already on the march. But the commander of their forces, General Mack, whose eagerness for battle with Napoleon was matched only by his incompetence, had overextended himself in the west. He could not wait for the Russian army to join him before attacking Napoleon. The French, moving much faster than expected, attacked and encircled Mack's forces at Ulm (October 1805). In a victory more famous than Marengo (as Napoleon had predicted it would be), Napoleon put out of commission an Austrian army of eighty thousand at small cost to himself. It was one of the greatest military victories in history, obtained within three weeks of crossing the Rhine and leaving France.

After the battle, Napoleon conversed with Mack, who said, "Your Majesty has troops marching through Switzerland, whose neutrality we have respected."

Napoleon: "*I* have not recognized its neutrality; consequently, I have a right to enter its territory."

Mack: "Ah! We are always the dupes of our good faith! And in the same way Your Majesty has violated the neutrality of Prussia. And yet, if I had wished to violate Prussian territory, I could easily have cut off the Bavarians' [Napoleon's allies] retreat!"

Napoleon smiled contemptuously, as if looking at a conscientious boy scout instead of the general of an army in combat.

.   .   .

***General Mack surrenders his Austrian army to Napoleon at Ulm,
October 1805.***

Napoleon's army next entered an abandoned Vienna. A month later, the Austro-Russian army, after various retreats, decided to stand and fight, especially as Prussia, another large, Germanic state stupidly decided at this late date to join the coalition. Now it was the czar's turn to be overeager, vain, and incompetent—dangerous things to be when facing Napoleon. Instead of waiting for the Prussian forces to join the Austro-Russian ones, the czar rushed to battle with Napoleon. The result was the battle of Austerlitz, in which Napoleon again waited patiently for the enemy commanders to make mistakes he could exploit (and by making a feint to the right, he kindly helped them err). It was in some ways an even greater victory than Ulm. The French, with only slight losses, put nearly fifty thousand enemy soldiers out of action in less than a day.

The Austrian Emperor Francis, beaten by Napoleon for a third time in a brief period, humbly asked for an interview, while the Russian czar, who in the vanity of youth had started the war and insisted on this battle, lost his nerve completely. He fled from the battlefield, accompanied by only one servant. When he thought himself safe, he got off his horse—and then broke down. Behold the great Czar of All the Russias, the Lord's Anointed, sitting alone by the side of a road and weeping like a child. The poor czar just barely missed being captured by the pursuing French.

Austerlitz was the most decisive of Napoleon's victories and one of the climaxes of his military career. It was in good part due to the fact that the Grand Army was the most powerful military instrument that he ever had. "I had the best army that ever was." It differed markedly from the Army of Italy with which he had first made his mark. That had been an undisciplined and demoralized army of volunteers owing allegiance to a republic governed by a squabbling committee, the Directory. The Grand Army owed its allegiance to a military genius who had hand-picked and trained it himself, who was also the ruler of his country with vast powers, and who could therefore

Napoleon receives the keys to Vienna, 14 November 1805 (detail).

dictate that all resources of the state be directed to whatever military campaign he planned.

The Russian forces now marched home, and Austria soon signed the humiliating peace treaty of Pressburg, in which she had to give up her last foothold in southern Germany and in Italy, as well as large sums of money. In a matter of weeks, Napoleon, with a masterful, quick march from the Rhine to the Danube, the destruction of the Austrian army, the capture of Vienna, and the severe defeat of the Russian army, had broken up the recently formed Third Coalition. Nearly unprecedented as his military achievements had been until now, Napoleon outdid himself in winning such massive triumphs over two emperors. From having consolidated his power at home and risen to ever greater political heights, perhaps the greatest that anyone had ever known, Napoleon had now returned to the place of the origin of his greatness, the battlefield, and risen equally in achievement there. Here in late 1805 is another of those climaxes of his career, as, at thirty-six, he was a general with a unique military record, not to mention Emperor of the French and King of Italy.

Another result of Austerlitz, however, was to confirm Napoleon in his belief that one big military victory solves all problems. By reenforcing his endless quest for conquests, that oversimplification, although understandable in 1805, did as much as anything to make him lose contact with reality and bring about his downfall.

Never one to be distracted from the sideshows by events in the main arena, Napoleon worked concurrently at building up the Grand Empire by picking up the pieces from a shattered Europe. Italy, long the battleground for the struggle between France and Austria, had been drawn in again by the resumption of war. Having already made himself king of the northern region, Napoleon turned south, where the king and queen of Naples had been a thorn in his side. In the wake of Austerlitz, he simply declared that the dynasty of Naples had ceased to

CAMPAIGNS IN
CENTRAL EUROPE
1805-7, 1809, 1813

100 mi
100   200   300 km

Niemen R.
Tilsit

BALTIC SEA

Königsberg
Friedland •
• Eylau

PRUSSIA

Elbe River

★ Berlin

Warsaw ★

N

Leipzig
Auerstadt • Lützen
Erfurt • Jena

Bautzen
• Dresden

AUSTRIA

• Austerlitz

Danube River
• Eckmühl
Ulm Landshut

Wagram
Aspern & Essling
★ Vienna

exist and sent his oldest brother Joseph to seize the city and be crowned king of the Two Sicilies.

In Germany, where Prussia and Austria competed for influence over the hundreds of small states, Napoleon encouraged territorial and constitutional changes that were offensive to the conservatism of the two monarchies. Then in July 1806, he officially abolished the antiquated thousand-year-old Holy Roman Empire by his own decree and established what he was pleased to call a Confederation of the Rhine. It consisted of the various states, fiefs, and principalities that separated themselves from dependency on either Austria or Prussia and put themselves under his protection. United with the kingdom of Westphalia, it was to be a third German-speaking power to rival Prussia and Austria. At the same time it would form, with France, the Low Countries, Switzerland, and Italy (and later he hoped, Spain) an Empire of the West. In return for his staying out of their internal affairs (at least for now), he expected the Confederation to be a steady source of money and troops, a military base for attack on Prussia or Austria, a buffer against Austria and Prussia if they ever attacked first, and, perhaps most important to a policy of divide and conquer, a stimulant to greater rivalry and friction between Austria and Prussia.

Francis, under pressure from Napoleon, removed his title of Holy Roman Emperor and had to settle for being allowed to remain known as just plain old Emperor of Austria. Had there ever been in European or even world history a man who made and unmade empires and kingdoms, princes and dukes, as if he were playing chess or cleaning out his desk?

Another piece Napoleon picked up as a by-product of the gigantic victories in central Europe were the ports on the North and Baltic seas. While busy fighting the great land powers, Napoleon was aware that his ultimate enemy was Britain— remote, cunning mistress of the seas, using her wealth to get other countries to do her fighting on land. After occupying the northern harbors in November 1806, he thought to strike hard at Britain. He declared her to be in a state of blockade. This "Continental System," as it was called, was meant to cut off all trade between Britain and the many countries under French control.

With her command of the oceans and her limited resources at home, Britain was heavily dependent on her overseas trade. The closing of foreign ports to her goods could have a catastrophic impact on the flow of money she needed to pay off her enormous national debt, to arrange the coalitions against Napoleon, and to subsidize continental armies. This act of his was really more of a boycott than a blockade, as the British were the ones good at blockading. It was merely Napoleon's retort to a blockade begun by Britain in November 1792 against Revolutionary France and revived in May 1806. The escalation continued on both sides throughout 1807. Napoleon hoped that, until or instead of an invasion of the large island, the dislocations resulting from his Continental System would bring a disunited Britain—perhaps even one racked by a French-style revolution—to her knees. It was also supposed to have the side effect of encouraging the growth of French industries to replace the imports.

Meanwhile, back in Central Europe, great as the military achievements of 1805 were, they were matched—unbelievably—by those of the following year. If 1805 was the Year of Austria (and Russia), 1806 was the Year of Prussia. Prussia had been the traditional ally of France even as Austria had been her traditional enemy. The Prussian King Frederick William admired Napoleon but was weak and indecisive. For his part, Napoleon was unable to respect anyone he did not fear, and so he was able to treat Prussia with contempt. The Prussian king came more under the influence of his wife and of the czar, who now hated Napoleon like the plague. Secretly negotiating with Russia, Prussia drifted toward war with France. She officially joined the Coalition just as that alliance started to come apart, two weeks after Ulm.

Napoleon enters Berlin, August 1806.

In any group, some people are always slow to get the word, read the handwriting on the wall, see what is under their noses. They may not be stupid, but they certainly are not bright. This was the role of the Prussians in 1805–6. Having erred twice in 1805 in not joining Napoleon when they could have, and then not joining Russia and Austria when they gathered their forces, Prussia erred again now in joining Napoleon's enemies in 1806 at the worst possible time and when his Grand Army was still in Germany. It was their turn to be overeager and incompetent, as General Mack and Czar Alexander had been. They took on Napoleon all alone, just when the Russian and Austrian forces were home nursing their wounds and counting their vast losses and when Napoleon was at the peak of his military achievements and fame. The only appropriate word for their action is "suicide." What the Prussians, with their antiquated institutions and army, expected to accomplish is anyone's guess. An elderly midget was challenging the heavyweight champion of the world.

Napoleon's strategic plan for beating this new foe is one of the masterpieces of the military art. Still, when the armies met, the Prussian soldiers managed to give a good account of themselves. Their poor leadership, however, enabled Napoleon, despite errors and unnecessary risks of his own, to win two big battles on the same day (August 13, 1806) at Jena and Auerstadt. The Prussians wore splendid uniforms and performed spectacular maneuvers, "but I soon taught them that to fight and to execute dazzling maneuvers were very different matters." The result was the French capture of Berlin, the surrender of the remaining Prussian forces, and the imposition on Prussia of a large war tax. Overnight, its once feared army wiped out, much of Prussia was in French hands. In one day's fighting, Napoleon had turned Prussia into what he had always suspected her to be, a second-rate power.

Napoleon spent a month in Berlin, where he was well received by the German populace. He paid homage to the tomb of Frederick the Great, the king who for a while, a generation or two earlier, had made Prussia a military power and whom Napoleon naturally revered. And, as usual, he saw to it that many great works of art were shipped back to Paris.

Napoleon next passed through Warsaw and defeated the Russian army in two separate battles on the same day in December 1806. Then at Preussisch Eylau (February 1807) there was fought one of the bloodiest battles history had yet seen. At one point, the French troops ran away, and Napoleon "won" only because in the end he, rather than the enemy, kept possession of the field. Despite this closing sour note, he had, for someone at war with Austria, Prussia, Russia, and Britain on fronts stretching all across Europe, achieved quite a track record during the past year and a half.

Napoleon began to weary of the campaign of 1806–7. His bulletin after Eylau spoke movingly of the thousands of corpses lying in the snow: "A sight such as this should inspire rulers with the love of peace and the hatred of war." After all his victories, he still faced many difficulties, and he had to resort to other strong measures to bolster his conquests. He accelerated the yearly call-up of new soldiers. He held out the promise of independence to the Poles if they turned against Russia. He dangled provinces before the sultan if Turkey joined the war on his side. Signing a treaty with Persia against Russia and Britain, he urged the Persians to seize the Russian province of Georgia.

Meanwhile, he continued campaigning, with mixed results. At Heilsberg, in June 1807, he violated his own key principle of always using all available forces in a major battle. Fighting with half his forces, he suffered a major setback. But, coming out of the battle still possessing numerical superiority, he fought again four days later. At Friedland, he dealt the Russians a severe blow. This was soon followed by the French seizure of Königsberg, the second most important city in Prussia.

96

Napoleon meets Czar Alexander I on a houseboat in the Niemen River, near Tilsit, 25 June 1807.

Some historians see in Napoleon's victories so far a lot of good luck, mainly in the form of errors made by his enemies. Only at Friedland, they say, was victory due to Napoleon's genius alone. From here on in, luck was not so much with him, and his genius would have to make or break him on its own. Napoleon himself declared Friedland to be as decisive a victory as Marengo, Austerlitz, and Jena, for this latest defeat made even the czar see the need for peace.

A truce was declared.

On the Russian border at Tilsit, in June 1807, Napoleon met with Czar Alexander on a sort of houseboat in the Niemen River. The Russian entourage was on one bank, and the French on the other. At a prearranged time, some men played trumpets and drums and others fired cannons, to signal the movement of monarchs. From either bank, a highly adorned boat set out, with numerous rowers. In the center of each sat the supreme ruler of his vast, powerful empire. The rowboats reached the houseboat at nearly the same moment. Each ruler stepped out, and the Czar of All the Russias formally greeted the Emperor of the West.

They stepped into the tent on the raft. No one else was present—no minister, interpreter, or servant. This was a conference between the leaders of what Napoleon called the two most powerful nations in the world.

Napoleon and Czar Alexander got along well. The Frenchman thought that the czar, with his wit, grace, charm, education, and subtlety, "may go far." Their nations' interests coincided as well—at least for a while. Both Russia and France needed peace and chafed under British sea power. Napoleon even spoke of a joint Russo-French expedition to take India from Britain. They behaved as though Europe was theirs to be divided into two spheres of influence or as though they were coemperors of the western and eastern portions of the ancient Roman Empire in its later stages. In the peace treaty that resulted in July, Prussia lost large portions of land, and secret

Napoleon meets Queen Louise of Prussia in Tilsit, July 1807. After admiring him, she eventually turned against him.

clauses potentially pitted Russia against Britain, and France against Turkey.

Despite the realization that Britain was still unbeaten, the ending of hostilities on the continent at least brought joy to France. Now Napoleon could concentrate on bringing all of Europe into his Continental System against Britain. The war with Britain had turned out to be the unplanned occasion—or was it just a pretext?—for Napoleon's land victories. The conquest of Europe was in part a by-product, it would seem, of the need to plug the leaks in the Continental System blockade. For, at the end of 1807, the Napoleonic Empire was at its height, and Napoleon nearly lord of Europe. Victor over all land powers, possessing an army of one million men, ruling from Hamburg to Rome, he was at another of those peaks in his career.

At this point, however, the decline that accompanies extreme success becomes visible. In Greek tragedy, a basically good man in a position of great power comes crashing down, often as a result of hubris, that is, swollen pride or vanity and consequent loss of contact with reality. The cause is explained by a famous dictum: "Power tends to corrupt, and absolute power corrupts absolutely." All great men have succumbed to it to some degree, and if anyone ever had absolute power, it was Napoleon.

Napoleon was in some ways a decent man who made many constructive contributions to society; he was able to carry his career through to the end; and he was a genius. He thus went further in positive achievements than almost anyone else in history. But even he lost his bearings. Although he often blamed subordinates for setbacks, and, in more philosophic moods, he blamed his failure on nature (the sea, the Russian winter) rather than on men, the truth is that no one—not Czar Alexander nor Wellington nor Blücher nor Talleyrand nor nature—defeated Napoleon. No one could. Ultimately, he defeated himself. His was, in fact, the classic example in history of what Greek tragedy was about.

Historians also play the game of trying to pinpoint the date or occasion when Napoleon's mind shows a slowing down and his character a decline, when open-mindedness and energetic inquiry are replaced by arbitrariness and intolerance of opposing views, when pipe dreams eclipse shrewd perceptions. Some pick 1805, the period of the coronations, of the fantasies of empire and aristocracy, of the encroachments on French liberty. Others point to 1807 and to Tilsit, when power went to his head; when egotism, in the form of vanity, pride, self-worship, psychic blindness, got out of control.

He now ignored the principles of the Revolution he stood for as a young man. His interests diverged from France's, and he no longer championed the continent against Britain. Consciously or unconsciously, his boundless ambition made him fight for the mastery of Europe, not for the sake of peace but for power for its own sake, for his own sake. He enriched France at the expense of Europe and his family at the expense of France. He made and unmade states, forcing on them constitutions without regard to local tradition, language, culture, or politics, without regard to popular feeling or national ideals. He seemed to feel himself above mere diplomacy and negotiations; he came to scorn compromise and moderation as useless. He grew incapable of having men with their own ideas around him. Losing awareness of how people felt about things, he became dangerously sure of himself. Becoming physically overweight—he who had been marked by extreme thinness—was curiously symbolic of his moral obesity, his increasing psychological thick-headedness. His growing belief that God or Destiny gave him the will and the force to overcome all obstacles was leading him into gross errors.

Such a blindness was at work in his Continental System. Napoleon ignored the fact that to many Europeans it was just another device for draining money from them and humiliating even allies and brothers. Closed to advice, he could not foresee that the attempt to tighten the screws on Britain with completion of the System had the undesirable side effect of bringing him into conflict with two of the strongest forces in Europe—the old Catholic Church and the new nationalism—and would lead him into losing struggles with Spain, the papacy, and Russia. Nor did he calculate that, as the French invasions of Spain and Russia were to prove, sometimes the more land one wins, the more vulnerable one becomes.

That the Continental System, like the struggle with the pope, came at the same time that he was taking the last steps in establishing a new nobility at home might make an outside observer fear for the future. Indeed the thought now occurred to some men very close to the emperor that he was perhaps no longer quite in his right mind. No wonder that two of his most important and shrewdest ministers, Talleyrand and Fouché, began to look beyond Napoleon. Talleyrand, a brilliant if erratic politician and diplomat who came from one of the oldest aristocratic families, had seen in 1797 that Napoleon was the coming man and had hitched his star to the general's wagon. Ten years later, however, he thought that Napoleon was unstable and should be removed. Others around the throne were coming to similar conclusions or at least growing uneasy. One of them said, "The Emperor is mad and will destroy us all."

CHAPTER SEVEN

The Beginning of Resistance

(*1808–1809*)

I f late 1807 and early 1808 saw Napoleon and the French at the summit of their power, the British by contrast felt isolated and besieged. The Russians were on Napoleon's side. Austria and Prussia were once again weak. The British economy was in dire straits. Fearing that Denmark might join the French, Britain decided on the drastic and much criticized step of bombarding neutral Copenhagen and seizing the Danish fleet. The immediate results only worsened Britain's predicament: Denmark rushed into the French camp; Russia was outraged; Prussia yielded to Napoleonic threats and joined the Continental System. The conditions of 1805, when France faced a grand coalition, were reversed, as Britain faced a newly united Europe.

All that was left was Portugal, by tradition a British ally. Now it was Napoleon's turn to try a bold step that would eventually boomerang. To complete the Continental System, the harbors of Portugal had to be controlled, and between France and Portugal lay Spain. The emperor presented Portugal with an ultimatum, threatening to join Spain in carving up that country. A French force marched through Spain and, in terrible shape, reached a Lisbon deserted by its rulers. The French had entered Spain supposedly on their way to conquering Portugal and to aid the Spaniards, but in reality it was to occupy, annex, and turn Spain into a Bonapartist kingdom. The truth became apparent in the spring of 1808, when the French army seized four major Spanish strongholds and a representative of Napoleon marched on Madrid.

For once Napoleon had undertaken a military campaign with little forethought. He who had been a general carefully conducting wars for the defense and well-being of France was more and more becoming an adventurer recklessly starting wars for the greater glory of himself. The attempt to seize Portugal embroiled him with the Spaniards far beyond his expectations. Spain had been allied with Revolutionary France and subservient to Napoleonic France, but neither nation approved of the other's form of government. The march to Portugal coincidentally gave Napoleon a chance to set the Spanish house in order to his liking.

The politics of the Spanish royal family were so intricate as to be a comedy. Napoleon, as was his habit, cut the knot directly. Forcing the various incompetent Bourbon claimants to the throne to resign, he imprisoned them. He then replaced them with his brother Joseph, who had been successful at Naples as King of the Two Sicilies. Napoleon planned thereby to bring to Spain the modernizing reforms he had brought to France, Italy, Egypt, Switzerland, and other smaller places. He thought of Spain as a land sunk in sloth, superstition, injustice, awful administration, and of its people as brutalized by the Inquisition, the nobility, the Churchmen, ignorance, and feudal tyranny. He would be the one to bring them something better.

Unlike the docile acceptance he found in other countries, however, Napoleon here ran into a hornet's nest. He had wrongly assumed that there was a large middle class in Spain that would welcome French-type reforms. He miscalculated the mood of the Spaniards because he was no longer the shrewd politician in contact with current trends. The pressure Napoleon brought to bear on the rulers of Spain led, on May 2, 1808, to a spontaneous rebellion in Madrid on the part of a Spanish people long outraged over their nation's subordination to the atheistic (as it seemed), revolutionary, imperialistic nation next door. The ruthlessness with which the French put down the rising merely fanned the flames of hatred and resolve. Something big had begun, something that would turn Spain into a widespread and perennial battlefield. Though the Spanish leaders and politicians, at least, acknowledged Napoleon's brother, Joseph, to be King of Spain, his authority existed only where there were French troops. Rebellions against the French broke out all over Spain.

Napoleon, for the first time, faced a united people waging a people's war. Many of his cherished notions bit the dust, among them that, once you beat a nation's leaders and army, you control the populace; another was that, once you capture the capital, which is the nerve center of government, you have the country. He had deposed the Spanish rulers and captured Madrid, but he had not much else. Large sections of Spain were angered that kingship should go to a Frenchman, a man from a country that persecuted the Church and was receptive to dangerous new ideas, and that would impose centralization on a country with strong traditions of local and provincial independence. All this Napoleon could not understand, so he went from one mistake in Spain to another. He was the very man who had said that Spain would be no problem: "I know

THE PENINSULAR WAR
1808-1814

the situation, and nothing that has occurred has been a surprise to me." It was a remark of sheer blindness and arrogance.

Several French forces suffered defeat or, what was worse, surrendered, perhaps because Napoleon was not present in person. The shameful French surrender at Baílen in July 1808 was notorious throughout Europe. An Austerlitz in reverse, it ended the myth of French invincibility. Although it had been a relatively minor skirmish, it made Napoleon suddenly seem vulnerable. Europe buzzed, with Austria and Prussia especially aroused for renewed combat. Though overt rebellion was brought under control for a while, Joseph had a terrible time trying to rule a hostile populace. Their spirit was strengthened by hatred of the viciously repressive French troops and by patriotic pride in the French defeat at Baílen.

Napoleon was still dreaming vaguely of a conquest of India, while forces were gathering in nearby Spain and Portugal that would bring him back to stern reality. Spanish appeals for help were listened to by a Britain delighted over Napoleon's unexpected embarrassment. A force was sent to Portugal, which included Arthur Wellesley who, years later as the Duke of Wellington, would help beat Napoleon for good.

If the campaign against Spain and Portugal (known as the Peninsular War) was really undertaken for the sake of Napoleon's Continental System, it proved to be monumentally counterproductive. Things would have been far simpler had Napoleon, not burdened with visions of omnipotence and world conquest, written off Spain and closed the short and easily patrolled Pyrenees frontier to British goods.

More important, the spontaneous Spanish nationalistic movement against a French invader was to spread to the Tyrol and later to Austria, Russia, and Prussia. Repeated in enough countries, this infectious patriotic zeal would undo the Napoleonic Empire. Italy and Germany were collections of independent states, but Spain had more of a unity and a national consciousness than they did. It was therefore unlike anything

Napoleon had confronted, and it became a role model for the nationalist movements springing up everywhere in Europe in its wake. From his earlier handling of insurrections in Paris, Cairo, and elsewhere, Napoleon had concluded that popular movements are shallow and easily stopped with the first show of force. He did not therefore understand the full scope of what was happening in Spain (and Austria and, in a sense, later in Russia) and thought that an army or two could quickly end matters.

His misreading of the Spanish challenge was aided by the fine results of his brief winter campaign there in late 1808 and by the contempt he had for the Spanish people, whom he considered "vile," "cowardly," barbarous, half-savage, superstitious, and more remote from civilization than even the Russians. After having fought and roundly beaten dynastic monarchies with their armies of hired soldiers, he faced something new— the enthusiasm of a whole people. He was great at dealing with generals, diplomats, kings and politicians, but not with masses of people. This ineptness actually increased when he became emperor, turned more conservative, and lost all touch with the day-to-day life and thought of average people.

Rushing to Spain in November 1808 to bring it into line, Napoleon took personal command of a large French army. He quickly won a series of victories in Napoleonic fashion and raced to Madrid, which surrendered without a fight. He planned to go right on to Lisbon, but, on hearing that British troops were in Salamanca, decided to beat them first. His army now had to proceed in terrible winter weather, and even soldiers marching near the emperor were heard to grumble.

Suddenly, on New Year's Day, 1809, Napoleon gave up the personal pursuit of the British and left the Spanish campaign in the hands of his generals. He had just received two sinister bulletins from Paris: Austria was on the move again; Talleyrand and Fouché, his two key ministers, becoming convinced that Napoleon was rushing to self-destruction and eager to

The Emperor commands.

prepare for any emergency in a state dependent on one precarious life were intriguing with one of his leading generals
over a successor. Prompted by his recurring sense of political
insecurity at home, Napoleon abruptly departed from Spain.

Although he could not have known it then, he forfeited possible victory there and opened the floodgates of disaster.

The gigantic fiasco looming in Spain was the direct result of Napoleon's attempt to perfect the Continental System in order to beat Britain and be master of Europe and probably the world. His obsession with the Continental System—or with power—also led to direct clashes with the very Catholic Church with which he had made his peace earlier, and to later clashes with Russia.

Napoleon's relations with Pope Pius VII had degenerated after the Concordat, as the emperor needled and harassed the pope with petty demands. Napoleon claimed that the pope was a spiritual leader only, not a political one, while the pope claimed that Napoleon was emperor of the French only, not of Rome. Napoleon saw himself as the lord of Rome, the Church as a department of the French Empire, the pope and bishops as his "moral prefects" or local governors. He acted as though he were the emperor of the Church and the pope were only the ruler of a small area known as the Papal States. He did not understand that millions of people the world over saw the Papal States and the temporal (worldly, political) power of the pope as a guarantee of his spiritual independence and leadership. In short, this was, on the emperor's part, a foolish struggle in which no money or territory or political power was at stake, but only his monumental, all-devouring ego.

The pope therefore refused to participate in the coronation of Napoleon as King of Italy in Milan in May 1805. When two years later Napoleon wanted a promise that the pope would be an ally of France, the pope, fearful that this would make the Vatican a servant of the emperor, again refused. The pope thus provided the biggest opposition Napoleon had yet run into. Their struggle escalated bitterly in 1808–9, at the very time when Napoleon was also undertaking the conquest of the most Catholic nation in Europe, Spain.

Insisting on imposing the Continental System on all Italy, Napoleon occupied Rome. The pope reacted by twice excommunicating Napoleon at inopportune times for the emperor, who was in the field preoccupied with his military campaigns and between major battles. In reprisal, Rome was incorporated into the French Empire; Napoleon's heir would in the future be called the king of Rome, and the emperor would be crowned in both Paris and Rome.

Napoleon especially resented the excommunication. He felt it was a political weapon used by a political pope, and he reacted in the spirit of one involved in a political struggle for power here and now. "This instant I have received the news," he announced in a mixture of anger, sarcasm, and mischievous glee, "that the Pope has excommunicated all of us. By this he has excommunicated himself. No more regard for him! He is a raving madman and must be locked up." A priest preaching war rather than peace, he announced, was abusing his role and "must be arrested."

A general promptly led a detachment of troops to Rome and at 2:00 A.M. forced his way into the pope's chambers. He asked the Holy Father to submit to the emperor's terms.

The pope responded in polite but firm words: "My son, I cannot, I must not, and I will not do so."

"Then I must put you under arrest."

The pope was immediately taken to France. The manner of his treatment and his physical suffering shocked all Europe, Protestant as well as Catholic. Even Napoleon, for once, was on the defensive. He claimed repeatedly—and insincerely—that he had wanted only a cardinal arrested, not the pope. Soon, though, he declared angrily that the pope would never return to Rome. He would find out much later that he had spoken too quickly.

In France, Napoleon had the pope cut off from all contact with the world. Ironically, that solitary confinement later prevented the pope from investing the bishops Napoleon appointed.

. . .

Things had certainly changed since the happy days of the Concordat, when Napoleon was looked upon by many, including the pope, as the restorer of the Catholic faith in France. Napoleon later forced the pope, a prisoner then at Fontainebleau, to sign a new Concordat even more favorable to the secular state. For Napoleon's need to conquer and dominate did not end with the political realm: "I would have become the master of the religious as well as of the political world." He had plans to convene Church councils, chair their deliberations, and approve their decisions "as did Constantine and Charlemagne."

Yet Napoleon claimed to have ambitious plans for the pope as well. After stripping him of all temporal power, he wanted to exalt the spiritual side, with pomp and ceremony. "I would have made an idol of him. He would have resided near me; Paris would have become the capital of Christendom." In such remarks, Napoleon appears to have begun confusing himself with God. And indeed he only half-jokingly regretted that, with nothing great remaining to be done, it was no longer possible in the modern world to do what Alexander the Great had done, proclaim himself the son of a god. For a ruler to be "adored like a god is as it ought to be!"

What with the war in Spain, the turbulence over papal power, and the renewed hostility of Austria and Prussia, continental Europe was far from the stable peace everyone thought existed in the wake of Tilsit a year earlier. Napoleon concluded that it was important to meet again with Czar Alexander, who had, with reason, grown reluctant. A second conference was held in September 1808 at Erfurt. A practical purpose for this meeting from Napoleon's viewpoint was to assure himself of a free hand for the campaign in Spain. The main, if unconscious motive, however, was to impress everyone with his own might and glory, to prove to France, to the czar, to the world, and, not least, to himself, that he was, as we would say, "the greatest."

For that purpose, all the conquered or satellite kings, princes, and dukes were "invited" by the French emperor to attend. The Erfurt conference, with its numerous ceremonial and social gatherings of Europe's ruling elite, has therefore been called a grand pageant, an international exposition, a world's fair, of the Napoleonic Empire.

At the business meetings, the two emperors in effect again planned to divide the world between them. But even here, beneath the imposing, glittering surface, cracks appeared. Napoleon's position was being undermined not only by events in Italy and Spain but also by very important men in his own entourage. Talleyrand, in particular, seeing the end of the line for Napoleon far down the road, secretly began to dissociate himself from his master. He offered Russian and Austrian officials his services in neutralizing the plans of the French emperor.

While Napoleon reveled in public displays of his greatness, a secret meeting took place between the czar and Talleyrand. The French minister urged the czar to save Europe—and France —by standing up to Napoleon, by being a mediator between France and Europe rather than an ally of France. He provided the czar with arguments, answers, and information to be deployed against the emperor. Above all, he said: "France is not interested in any conquests beyond the Rhine, the Alps, and the Pyrenees. The nation is civilized; her ruler is not."

Talleyrand was not only acting on his own behalf. He had his finger, as Napoleon no longer had, on the pulse of the people. According to one observer, in 1808 there were two parties in France: Napoleon, backed by some of his generals, wanting to extend his power in Europe; and the rest of France, fearful of losing all its gains. Napoleon and France were pulling in different directions. Erfurt was not like Tilsit. Napoleon no longer represented the will of France, as he always claimed to. He neither charmed nor intimidated the czar, and all Europe knew it.

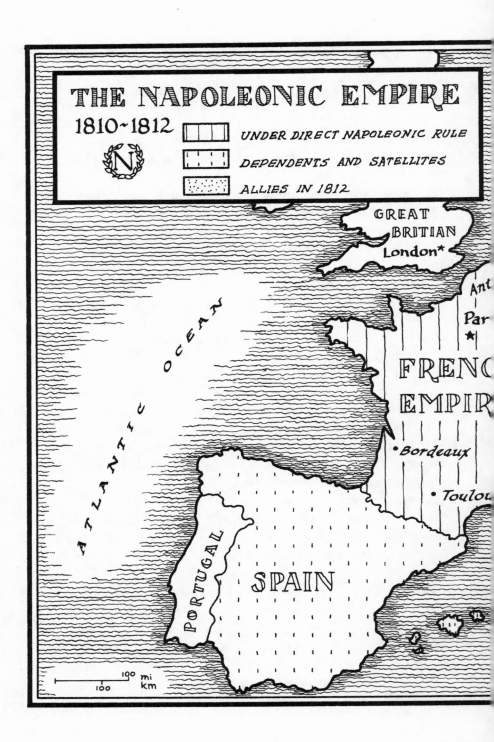

THE NAPOLEONIC EMPIRE

1810~1812

UNDER DIRECT NAPOLEONIC RULE

DEPENDENTS AND SATELLITES

ALLIES IN 1812

GREAT BRITIAN
London★

Ant

Par
★

FRENC
EMPIR

•Bordeaux

• Toulou

ATLANTIC OCEAN

PORTUGAL

SPAIN

100 mi
100 km

꧁꧁꧁꧁꧁꧁꧁꧁꧁꧁꧁꧁꧁꧁꧁꧁꧁꧁꧁꧁꧁꧁꧁꧁꧁꧁

CHAPTER EIGHT

Indian Summer and Gathering Clouds

(1 8 0 9 – 1 8 1 1)

The defeats of 1805–7 with their peace treaties of Pressburg and Tilsit impoverished and humiliated the
German-speaking peoples. In 1808, with Napoleon
deeply involved in Spain, the opportunity for retaliation seemed
at hand. Not just revenge was at stake but survival, for Napoleon was clearly out to rule Europe. The Emperor Francis was
particularly aroused by the dethronement of the Spanish Bourbons. The experience of Spain proved that compliance and
subservience were no guarantee against Napoleon's ambition
and ruthlessness.

But it was not just the Austrian monarch's reaction alone
that mattered anymore, as it had in the panic of the early 1790s
over the spread of the radicalism of the French Revolution.
Napoleon meant to destroy not only all the royal families, as

had the Revolution, but also regional self-government and local traditions.// The war that Austria began without allies against France in 1809 therefore had something new to it—great popular support. Patriotic writings abounded, and a national militia was easily formed. The principles of the Revolution, which Napoleon had spread so well throughout Europe, were arousing in the countries he had conquered the desire to be free from the very Frenchmen who had taught them such principles and desires. "Liberty" was something to be obtained as much by overthrowing a French prefect or general as a native monarch or nobleman. This is "nationalism," the sense among people speaking the same language that they belong to a single culture, tradition, and nation, which is, or should be, proud and independent. The same nationalism that first made Revolutionary France dynamic was caught by others and turned against Napoleon.

The French emperor had thought that divisions ran along class lines—middle class and peasant versus aristocrat—and that the destruction of the old dynastic regimes would establish common laws and like-minded people throughout the continent. What happened instead was that the overthrow of monarchies, together with Napoleon's own ambition and despotism, stimulated an awakening of national consciousness. During the years 1804–8, the European image of Napoleon changed from that of an enlightened reformer and liberator to that of a dictator, partly because of the ferment his own reforms had created, partly because of his personal turn to conservatism, and partly because of the inevitable oppressiveness of the conquerors.

Napoleon had instituted the Napoleonic Code in many parts of the Empire. The Code became the means of exporting not only the reforms of the Revolution (in their Napoleonic version) but also the heavy hand of French domination. In fact, the reforms came to seem like window dressing for the domination. "The annexed territories must be just like France," Napoleon advised a brother, "and if you went on annexing everything as far as Gibraltar and Kamchatka, the laws of France would have to spread there too." Europe needed a regeneration, he believed, something that could only be brought about by a "superior power," which would dominate the others and "force them to live in harmony with one another—and France is best placed for that purpose."

Thus it was that a unity came to be imposed on the various conquered territories as if they were a series of "departments" or states of France. The ruler was, directly or indirectly, Napoleon. Taxation and conscription impoverished the local peoples in order to serve the interests of France. As he often said and wrote, "My principle is France first" or "France before everything." He wanted a unified, liberalized, modern society not for the sake of local or national aspirations but for the sake of French needs. At no time does France "wage war for the sake of other nations. It is for France I have conquered Spain. I have conquered her so that she may be French."

No wonder that Napoleon complained that the Italians —who, like the Spaniards and others, had no inclination to be French—gave the liberty-bearing French little help. No wonder that the European peoples felt about Napoleon's policy as we would about having the laws of Iran or South Africa or Russia imposed on us, even if it were for our own good. We would revolt; so did they. Napoleon was absolutely right in believing that the French people would accept a conquering hero as a trade-off for their freedom. He forgot, however, that the non-French people might have a different view of their conqueror and that, if the conquests continued, there would eventually be a lot more of the conquered than of hero-worshipping Frenchmen. And once these people started fighting back together and winning, the French people too would no longer have a conquering hero to worship but a tyrant to resent.

In 1805, only the Austrian government wanted war with France. By 1808–9, the people and army wanted it as well, actually in advance of their government. This was not just another war but an entirely different kind of war. It was no longer the case of a conservative Hapsburg or Bourbon monarch defending himself against radical ideas or a Napoleonic usurper; rather all the Germanic or Spanish people were rebelling against the domineering French people. The new spirit in Austria was generated and aided by the earlier popular movement in Spain. The French military humiliation at Baílen further inspired the Austrian and Prussian nationalists. Part of Napoleon's tragedy is that he was oblivious to the new currents sweeping through Europe.

Another important impact that Napoleon unintentionally had was to bestir the Austrian bureaucracy into modernizing its army—along Napoleonic lines, of course. The man mainly responsible for that streamlining, the able Archduke Charles, soon took command of the troops in the field. Austria was ready and willing yet again to tackle the great Napoleon.

The eagerness was, for once, not mutual. The war of 1805 had been unpopular in France, and now in 1809 neither the people nor most of the generals, knowing the treasury to be half-empty and the army filled with raw conscripts and foreigners, were in a mood for a new war. Napoleon had few troops in Germany, as his main army was bogged down in Spain, from where he had just returned. He faced a renewed and more dangerous Austria, organized and enthusiastic, while a rebellious Spain, backed by Britain, was raging at his rear or flank. And how long could Russia and Prussia, humiliated by him before, be relied on to stay neutral when he was, or seemed to be, in serious trouble?

Worse even was the change in Napoleon himself. He seemed to lack his usual speed and dynamism. First he abandoned Spain without destroying the rebel and English forces there, and now he remained in Paris, busy with hunting and theater going, leaving command of his soldiers to an unimaginative subordinate. Had he come to believe so thoroughly in his destiny that he felt he need not exert himself? Or was he wearing out, aging? It was probably only a coincidence that when he finally came to the battlefield in Austria, he was hit in the ankle by a bullet, the only time in a military career filled with visits to flaming battlefields that he suffered physical injury. Yet one could be excused for seeing something ominous in a first injury at such a time.

To be sure, once he got going, he got going. Two hours after the Austrian declaration of war in April 1809, he was on the way to the front, and, in the battle that soon followed, the Austrians were outpaced and outfought by the French. From a situation of peril, Napoleon carried out some of his finest maneuvers and won a victory of quick improvisation over hesitating tactics by the enemy. In the wake of this victory at Eckmuhl and within weeks of the war's beginning, Napoleon again occupied Vienna. His quick defeat of the Austrians may have prevented the combative spirit from spreading to Prussia for this year at least.

Still, he faced a powerful foe now, and he suffered setbacks. For about two months, he was hemmed in, a long way from his capital, while the pope was excommunicating him, the British were plotting against him, the Spaniards rebelling, the Russians and the Prussians uncertain allies. In the battle of Aspern-Essling, near Vienna, Napoleon went into combat without knowing the enemy's dispositions, without securing passage of a river, and without concentrating his army. Confronting a force much larger than his own, he finally had to withdraw. Although both sides suffered vast casualties, the fact that he was not invincible created a sensation in Europe, because by now so much more was expected from Napoleon and his Grand Army. His present loss of face was, paradoxically, a tribute to his uniqueness. Nor was the Grand Army, its best parts wasting in Spain and its ranks diluted by many raw young conscripts, what it had been. News of the defeat of Aspern-Essling made people wonder if the end was near.

Luckily for Napoleon, the Austrians did not exploit their advantage. They remained uncoordinated, while Napoleon, as often, was at his best when in difficult straits. In a third big battle, near Wagram, the French again were not faring as of old. Napoleon ran out of reserves, and only his personal intervention saved the day.

The Austrians retreated in good order. Having made a good showing for two days against one of the greatest commanders of all time and having suffered fewer casualties than the French, they had only barely lost. The battle of Wagram,

Napoleon at the Battle of Wagram, July 1809.

which saw the greatest artillery battle yet known to history,
caused Napoleon to have a new respect for the Austrians. It
also prompted his somewhat uncharacteristic observation that
battle should be the last recourse because the outcome is always
uncertain.

During this period, nationalistic peasant risings in the
Tyrol (a province between Austria and Italy) swept out the
French and brought back the Austrians. When Napoleon decided to send in a strong French force, the rebellion spread, just
as had the one in Spain. For a while the Tyroleans stood off
the French troops. They finally succumbed, but, coming at the
same time as the defeat at Aspern-Essling and the costly victory
at Wagram, the rising left another chink in the French aura
of invincibility. With Austria stronger than it had been in
years and Prussia no longer docile, with Russia, Britain, Spain,
and Portugal restless, with men close to him intriguing against
him and his unpopular war, Napoleon now faced many potential dangers. Luckily, nothing serious happened then. While
he had his hands full with Spain and Austria, Britain tried to
gain advantage by supplying the Spaniards with money and
matériel, by reenforcing her small army in Portugal, and by
sending an expedition against Antwerp. The last venture
flopped, and the effects of the others took a while to be felt.

An armistice in July 1809 saved Napoleon from further
embarrassments. It was followed by the Treaty of Schönbrunn
(October 1809) which forced Austria, despite her impressive
comeback, to recognize the Bonapartist crowns of Italy and
Spain, to reduce her army, to give up much land and population, and to pay large sums, as well as the usual valuable manu-
scripts and art works.

Also unsettling at this time was an adolescent's attempted
assassination of Napoleon. The youth turned out not to be, as
Napoleon was eager to believe, a lunatic, but a proud, prin-
cipled martyr for German liberty acting against a tyrant. Napoleon was used to assassination attempts by Bourbon agents, but

not by an educated young man from a respectable middle-class clergyman's home. The incident was a clear sign that the new spirit in Europe was turning against Napoleon, hitherto seen as the champion of enlightenment and liberty.

Still ignoring the "grass-roots" basis of the recent movements against him, Napoleon thought to consolidate the peace with Austria by means of one of the oldest—and rapidly becoming archaic—diplomatic devices: dynastic intermarriage. He would marry an Austrian princess. But was there not a slight impediment to such an arrangement—his being already married to Josephine? Yes, but Napoleon had long been needing an heir, especially when he became a hereditary emperor. His present marriage was barren. His relations with his wife Josephine had had their ups and downs. At first he had been in love with her, then disillusioned on finding out that she had other lovers. Yet they remained together, and he became dependent on her, so much so that at his own coronation he had had her crowned as well. By now, however, the birth of several illegitimate children convinced him that the infertility of their marriage was due to her, not him. His need for an heir was, moreover, supplemented by the change taking place in his now imperial character. Regarding himself as at least as good as, if not downright superior to, the old ruling dynasties of Europe, he wanted a real princess for a wife, for the sake of his own ego, of his descendants, and of his nation.

In late 1809, Napoleon therefore dissolved the marriage to Josephine. The divorce violated two articles of his own imperial statutes and also required special permission from the pope. Since the pope had been interned by the French and was not likely to cooperate, Napoleon established a French ecclesiastical commission, which declared the marriage null and void. The constitutional barrier was taken care of by the rubber-stamp legislature. As one historian nicely puts it, the obsequious French senate decreed the marriage dissolved, and the bishop's court declared it had never taken place at all.

As early as 1807 Napoleon had already been looking over a list of eligible princesses and narrowed it down to a few imperial families, then to the Russian and Austrian ones. For a while the Russian option was attractive, but both sides held back. Concurrently, Napoleon and the Austrian government came to see the advantage of such a union as a way of cementing the recently restored peace. So, in the spring of 1810, Napoleon married Marie Louise, the daughter of Emperor Francis of Austria. The French people rejoiced over the likelihood of a royal heir and over what looked like an insurance policy covering the peace with Austria. How much greater was the joy of the once impoverished little Corsican adventurer who had come a very long way to find himself now in the proudest royal family in Europe, in the family of the famous Empress Maria Theresa and of Queen Marie Antoinette and Louis XVI.

Indeed, the arrival of Marie Louise in Paris speeded the reactionary trend that had replaced Napoleon's republican policy when he had been First Consul. More and more, heredity was taken into account rather than Napoleon's inspiring motto of "careers open to talent" irrespective of social origin. He paid less attention to popular opinion at home and drifted further away from the ideals of the Revolution. He made the French treasury pay the newly created aristocracy handsomely and pay far larger sums into his own pockets. He favored the old nobility of the ancient Bourbon regime, much sought after by the government now, rather than the middle class, although the Revolution had been made by the middle class against the monarchy. To marry the great-niece of Marie Antoinette was like a violation of the Revolution's basic principle. It was another wedge driven between himself and the growing number of disillusioned former supporters. The needs of his ego and of his empire building overruled his political sense. Napoleon's increasing conservatism paralleled his loss of contact with reality.

Before and after the wedding, Napoleon acted like a youth

Napoleon marries Princess Marie-Louise of Austria, 1810.

in love for the first time. He set aside all serious business, dressed neatly, lost weight, learned how to dance, and spent much time with the princess—who had neither physical beauty nor an interesting personality. All this at the very time that the war in Spain remained inconclusive and the menace in the East was growing. The Napoleon of 1805 would have quickly decided which problem to attend to first and whether to do so by force or by diplomacy. The Napoleon of 1810 was drifting.

Marie Louise slowly learned to like, even love, Napoleon, but his attachment to her lasted only until the birth of a child. Given the title King of Rome, this son was the long-awaited heir to the empire Napoleon had conquered and created. The birth of a son and the general rejoicing that followed seemed to jutsify his repudiation of a commoner wife and of the republican way of life. Despite forebodings about Spain and Russia, and French economic woes, the baptism of the boy may be seen as another climax of Napoleon's career, the zenith of his empire. For a brief interlude, Napoleon and France were still inseparably one. His regime seemed more secure than ever. Now at last the contented emperor threw himself back into his work with the zeal of the Napoleon of old.

In the wake of peace with Austria and his marriage, he turned his attention closer to home. He was almost master of continental Europe. Only Britain eluded his clutch—Britain, tantalizingly just a few sea miles beyond the reach of his Grand Army; Britain, which had neutralized the French and Spanish fleets and was stirring up Portugal and Spain; Britain, from the pursuit of which he had been distracted by the resurgence of Austria in January 1809 and once before, in August 1805. She had become France's archenemy, at least in the mind of its emperor: "England and France have held the fate of the earth in their hands. How much evil we have inflicted on each other. How much good we might have done!" As a good Frenchman, he hated those neighbors. "War to the death with England! Always—until she is destroyed!"

Throughout 1808–10, he strengthened the Channel ports, and in 1811 he reassembled the invasion flotilla of 1805. He still dreamed of naval superiority, especially as he had the whole coastline of Europe under his control. "Before ten years are up," he said, "We shall succeed. I shall conquer England." He even entertained a proposal to send an airborne military force, complete with artillery and horses, to Britain on hot air balloons, recently invented by the Montgolfier brothers. This did not, however, prove feasible.

Defeating this last enemy of his became the goal of all his policies, and, until he was ready to invade, tightening the Continental System became his main policy.

Napoleon was outraged that nearby Holland violated his boycott by continuing to trade with Britain. When he undertook punitive measures, his youngest brother, Louis, who as King of Holland looked after the welfare of his Dutch people, protested and resigned his throne. An angry Napoleon simply annexed the country. Greater France, "my federated states, or the true French Empire," now included the Low Countries (Holland and Belgium), the kingdoms of Italy and Naples, Switzerland, and the Confederation of the Rhine. Nearly all the countries of Europe were dependent on, or allied with, France, except for Russia and Britain at the perimeter. According to one computation, in 1810, seven kingdoms and thirty principalities (domains ruled by princes) were vassals of France.

Even Britain might now be vulnerable. In 1810, Napoleon thought that the Continental System was bringing her to collapse at long last. She was racked by financial crises, unemployment, popular discontent, aroused opposition in Parliament, even fears of a famine. The only trouble was that the French economy was hardly doing any better, and Napoleon, in order to raise tax money, allowed various loopholes in the system to be exploited.

So it was that the Continental System, which lasted for years, in the end proved to be a failure. Though it might have worked only over a long period, in practice it was applied only sporadically. Britain's growth in population and prosperity were not affected. The Industrial Revolution was an important new factor in Britain, which Napoleon did not take into account. And economic warfare by itself could not have secured a clear political decision. Instead of falling on each other's throats, the British social classes managed more or less to unite and see the thing through to victory. Napoleon had misread the strength of the British economy and, especially, the British character. //

Napoleon's undoing was, furthermore, caused by his attempt to perfect the Continental System, a project to which he devoted most of his attention in the two years after the victory at Wagram. The severe interruption of trade that it represented was now bringing economic hard times to Europe and, along with conscription, made Napoleon's rule very unpopular. It especially hurt the very middle class that would have been the most likely to respond to Napoleon's proclaimed values of enlightenment and equality. It lead to the miasma of Spain, the break with the pope, and war with Russia.

Of these three, Spain was the first to sap his power. As he went from triumph to triumph—victory over Austria, marriage and fatherhood, annexation of Holland, apparent strangulation of Britain—he was haunted by Spain, that festering sore, that incurable cancer. The Spain that he had abruptly left in early 1809 was in French hands in name only. By the end of the year, most of the land seemed to be again under French control, but the people were still unconquered.

Napoleon's generals were used, by training and experience, to dealing with professional soldiers massed in traditional formations and maneuvers as part of armies that could be traced, seen, trapped, and beaten by tactics of his (or their) devising. But Spain no longer had a formal army to speak of. In this new kind of war, the French faced informal guerrilla bands whose hit-and-run tactics were greatly dependent on

their knowledge of the terrain and their ties to the local populace. Now the initiative and the tactics were on the Spanish
side. The British, sending supplies and advisers, did their best
to keep it that way. Geographically, Spain was ideal for guerrilla
warfare and for the small land army of Britain to operate
in. Wellesley (Wellington-to-be) already had, with an Anglo-
Portuguese army, ejected the French from Portugal.

Napoleon conducted this unusual war from Paris or Germany rather than on the spot, thereby making things worse,
for local conditions changed rapidly, and, by the time his
instructions arrived, they were obsolete. It also did not help
that the Peninsular War was unpopular with the French soldiers. Used to fighting their professional counterparts, they now
faced ambushes by a hostile civilian population and by phantom
units. Used to fighting on behalf of the French Revolutionary
principle of liberty, they now seemed to be fighting *against* the
same principle as espoused by the Spanish people. Nor had they
any interest in whether Napoleon's brother got to keep the
Spanish throne.

Nor was there a Napoleon on horseback nearby on whose
behalf they could fight and in whose eyes they could gain
medals. First the war and the peace negotiations with Austria,
then preoccupation with tightening the Continental System,
then his marriage and the birth of his son, then the growing
friction with Russia—each prevented Napoleon from taking
charge of the Spanish campaign in person. Perhaps deep down
he also had no desire to involve himself in a war that held no
easy answers and that had a clear risk of failure.

Instead of finishing the job himself, Napoleon sent a hundred thousand veterans to Spain, thereby depleting his resources
for subsequent campaigns, a serious error. Another error was
to think that the job could be done, in lieu of his presence
there, by threats of annexing Spain and by atrocities committed by his army. The Spaniards, ever a proud people, were
merely further aroused against the French by these blows to

their dignity. Hence Spain was destined to become a quagmire for the French army.

Napoleon decided in the spring of 1810 to drive the British out of Portugal. The French, under General Masséna, faced stiff opposition from a well-fortified country. Given dictatorial powers by the Portuguese government, Wellesley had trained the local soldiers and civilians. He built a large series of lines of fortifications near Lisbon. He practiced a scorched-earth policy by destroying all the food and lodging in areas through which the French army would march.

Masséna urged Napoleon to come down; his presence would restore discipline among the generals and revive the spirit of the troops. Although Napoleon had said in 1803 that, because of faith in himself and in his lucky star, he counted on military victory only when "I myself am in command," he now was evasive. By May 1811, Masséna, defeated by Wellesley's diligence, by disease, and by dissension in the French camp, gave up the command. This confirmed the impression made by the surrender at Baílen that something was amiss with Napoleon and his Grand Army. Europe, especially Prussia, took note of this new sign that Napoleon could be beaten, and talk began of an all-European war of liberation against the French emperor.

After the failure of Masséna's expedition, the French kept three hundred thousand troops in Spain, but without coordination, plan, or determination. Napoleon appears to have seen the need to clear out, but lacked the will or courage to act. He left the army in Spain but weakened it by removing portions to other fronts when he should have either withdrawn completely or greatly reenforced it. The French generals there, in the absence of Napoleon's authoritative presence, quarreled with each other. The French soldiers, losing discipline and morale, misbehaved terribly.

The Peninsular War had the effect of raising British morale by enabling Britain to engage a large enemy force with a small army of her own and to achieve success on land at last.

In July 1812, Wellesley took the offensive and severely defeated the French at Salamanca and then entered Madrid to great acclamation. Although he left again at the approach of another French army, he had made his mark. Appointed commander in chief of all Spanish forces, he spent the winter of 1812–13 training an Anglo-Portuguese-Spanish army. In May 1813, he attacked and defeated the French at Vitoria. This action enabled him to cross the border into France and then defeat the French later at Toulouse. But by then, in April 1814, the French Empire was unravelling.

CHAPTER NINE

The Moscow Trip

(1 8 1 2)

If Napoleon's life is an epic tale, it contains within it numerous mini-epics—incidents that are rich and incredible enough to be each written up in a large volume of fiction. One such mini-epic is the story of his return to power after his fall. An earlier one is the invasion of Russia and the monumental five-hundred-mile expedition to Moscow, one of the great adventures in history.

While Napoleon was regularly able to tame the Central European land powers in a matter of weeks or months, he had been unable to conquer, even after years of hostilities, either Spain or Britain, two nations on the periphery of Europe and without large armies. Why a Napoleon preoccupied with an unfinished job in those two lands would try at the same time to conquer a huge country also on the periphery of Europe remains a mystery to this day.

The Treaty of Tilsit was never taken more seriously by either side other than as a stopgap measure. Many Russians thought it a humiliation. The treaty committed the czar to join Napoleon's Continental System. That policy was unpopular with the Russian people because being cut off from British trade resulted in serious financial difficulties. Popular pressure therefore made the czar withdraw from the Continental System at the very time that Napoleon, beginning to see a happy outcome, wanted to make it leakproof. Obsession with the system was bringing Napoleon in conflict with Russia even as it had with the papacy and, via Portugal, with Spain.

One of the ways Britain got around the boycott was to send many of her goods in ships from neutral countries. Napoleon's demand for a halt to such evasion led to friction. In December 1810, Czar Alexander officially opened his ports to neutral shipping and imposed high tariffs on French imports. This repudiation of the Continental System, forced on the czar by the Russian national interest, seemed to the egotistic Napoleon to be a personal rebuff, a sign that Russia would return to an alliance with Britain.

The economic factor was only one among many others. Perhaps it was a symptom of a larger cause, a struggle for the mastery of Europe between two superpowers, both of whom were eager to gain control of Turkish Constantinople (Istanbul) and the Dardanelles. Or maybe it was less a war between France and Russia than a personality clash between two proud autocrats who could not coexist; or a collision between a semi-insane man of strong will and the patriotism of an entire people.

Napoleon himself was not clear as to what he was trying to achieve with this war. At one point, he spoke, in what we would now call Hitlerian language, of finishing for good "the colossus of the barbarian North," of driving the Russian barbarians, slaves, and beasts back to their icefields and out of civilized Europe. Yet, a month later, he said, "I am only waging a political war against Alexander. We can soon agree if he will negotiate." This remark hardly sounds as if he were leading a crusade on behalf of civilization. Nor did he present himself (despite some talk later of emancipating the serfs) as leading a movement to liberate oppressed classes or subjects, as he had done in Italy and Germany.

Perhaps toppling Russia would be an answer to the critics of his invasion of Spain. Perhaps he thought that crushing the only remaining continental power that could cause trouble by joining Britain was a way of further isolating and destroying Britain. With the latter gone, Spain and the last resistance in Europe to him would quickly be finished. No less important was the romantic dream shimmering on the horizon beyond Moscow, the dream that had been haunting him since the Egyptian campaign, when he had begun to think of paralleling the amazing career of Alexander the Great and of marching to the Ganges River. "After all," he said about the way to Moscow, "that long road is the road to India."

Napoleon seemed to rely on luck more than ever. He was becoming irritable and less inclined to listen to advice. He began to change his foreign ministers often now, as the interests of France differed more and more from those of the Empire and of, especially, Napoleon. While all the men around him warned him of the many difficulties he faced in invading Russia and some were even working against him, he remained certain that a quick victory there would show Europe the futility of further resistance, close the gaps in the boycott, and cause Britain's downfall.

The abrupt breaking off of negotiations for a possible marriage to the czar's sister and his haste in marrying the Austrian princess were insulting to the czar. It did not so much contribute to the rift between the two nations as bring the rift into the open, symbolize it. If 1810 was the year of the decision, 1811 saw overt military preparations on both sides. The tone between the two emperors became accusatory. Napoleon secured his flanks by forcing an alliance on Prussia and

Austria in the spring of 1812. Russia stood alone, except for a Britain that was far away and of no help. Nevertheless, the czar was willing to take on the monster and fight a long war rather than see Russia dependent on France as were the Germanic states. When Napoleon seized the Swedish territory of Pomerania, near Russia, in April 1812, Russia presented France with an ultimatum.

Although Napoleon had prepared for an all-out war, he thought that he could force the czar into submission by a mere show of overwhelming power and, if that failed, with a prompt, definitive victory after the fashion of Austerlitz. As he liked to say: "One good battle will settle all that!" A big victory near the frontier at the beginning of hostilities followed by a peace dictated on his terms—that had worked for him so often in the past. "A battle is my plan of campaign, and success is my whole policy." Just as in the case of Britain and Spain, however, he had not appreciated the resourcefulness and determination of the populace. If his goal was to break his opponent's will, that will was actually hardened by partial defeat and by elusive victory, and the Russians could neither be bluffed nor beaten into surrender.

Napoleon's army in 1812 numbered over a million, one of the largest, most powerful in European history until then. Some half million of these were sent into the Russian campaign, with the accompanying huge accumulations of food supplies and transportation, and 250,000 of these were attack troops. This Grand Army, more than twice as large as the Russian army, was amazing even in that turbulent age of wars. It was actually the first campaign in which Napoleon had such a marked superiority of numbers. He was obviously taking no chances.

On the other hand, many of the old veterans were gone, and the rest were tired of wars that seemed to be fought only for the glory of Napoleon and his family. The departed veterans were replaced by untrained young men reluctantly drafted. A good half were foreigners, practically shanghaied into service, men with a deficient sense of mission and discipline. Napoleon brought into the expedition contingents from nearly every satellite country in Europe, not only to impress the world but also as hostages from the various peoples under the Napoleonic yoke. Many of the best French troops were serving in Spain.

If Napoleonic strategy was to engage the Russians as quickly and fully as possible in quest of a knockout blow and if he had such a vast numerical superiority, it would have been in Russia's interest to avoid battles by moving inland. Napoleon himself had taken admiring note in 1810 of Wellesley's scorched-earth policy in Spain, whereby the Englishman ruined an army he dared not fight. And Czar Alexander had likewise observed what had worked in Spain against the French—avoidance of big battles and retreats into the interior. This was indeed what eventually happened in Russia, but it did not result from any superior strategy or insight. On the contrary, the Russian generals were as deluded as General Mack, Czar Alexander, and the Prussians had been in previous campaigns. They were all too eager to fight Napoleon early rather than to retreat. They wanted a decisive victory at the border as much as Napoleon did. But, because of conflicting battle plans and the absence of a single supreme commander, confusion reigned in the Russian camp in the face of the approaching juggernaut. And so, by default, against their wisdom, and despite themselves—they stumbled into the right strategy.

Finally, supreme command was given to General Kutuzov, who was temperamentally inclined to patient delaying of a battle until the conditions were ripe for it. Here was a situation in which Napoleon did not want to penetrate deeply and most of the Russians did not want to retreat deeply, but depth is what both sides got. The main factor in the war became, at least for the French, not massacres but supply lines.

On the way to the front, Napoleon stopped at Dresden, where all the monarchs and rulers of Central Europe came to pay homage to him as they had at Erfurt a few years before. Then, on June 24, 1812, he sent his vast force across the Niemen River border into Russia.

Facing two wings of the Russian army, he expected, as usual, to beat one and then destroy the other. The Russians, eager for a battle, waited for a favorable opportunity. Given the vast French numerical superiority, such opportunities were not exactly plentiful. So the Russians learned, against their will, the virtues of patience and procrastination. They became adept at, got into the habit of, evading the Grand Army.

Though the French fought no battle, conditions soon deteriorated for them. First they were oppressed by heat, thirst, and dusty roads. The heavy rains that then came took care of those problems only to raise new ones: the roads became muddy, and the flow of supplies was interrupted. This led to straggling and looting that corroded army discipline, alienated the populace, and made the French seem like gangsters rather than liberators. Because the retreating Russian army had already passed through earlier and laid waste to much of the land, the marauding French had to extend laterally for many miles. The death of huge numbers of horses from hunger soon crippled the supply lines even more and led to greater starvation. Before fighting a single battle, the French lost more men from hardship, breakdown of discipline, desertion, and illness than if they had fought. The loss of twenty thousand horses and almost a hundred thousand soldiers was wastage equivalent to at least two big battles. Napoleon had nothing to show for these statistics except long marches through enemy territory. He grumbled often now, and his bulletins were full of lies.

June 26. Napoleon entered Vilna, the first major Russian city, and sent offers of peace to the czar. The courier was taken to the large ornate audience hall in the Kremlin, where the czar sat in imperial splendor on a throne on a dais, surrounded at a lower level by his advisers and his nobles. A counsellor read

aloud the message from Napoleon. When he finished, silence
descended on the hall. After an interlude, Alexander, Czar of
All the Russias and the Lord's Anointed, rose slowly and, on
the dais, towered over the scene. He began softly, but as he
proceeded, his voice rose to a crescendo: "You may inform
your Emperor that, as God is my creator and judge, Christ my
redeemer, and Holy Russia my witness, I swear by all the power
in my body and in my eternal soul that I will never negotiate

as long as a *single* French soldier stands on holy Russian soil. *Never!"* As if at a signal, all the advisers waved their fists and yelled, "Never!"

A few days later, after Napoleon was given a detailed description of the incident by the courier, he smiled.

The French wasted two and a half precious weeks in Vilna waiting for a peace move. But the "sole sight of the unprecedented armaments" of the French did not by itself budge the czar, as Napoleon thought it might.

July 24. At the next major city, Vitebsk, the French stopped for two more weeks. A complete review of their situation was called for. The marching capacity of the troops had proved to be nowhere near what Napoleon had expected because he had not taken into account what they would be up against. Having obtained much of his military experience in Italy and Germany, where the armies had been smaller, the countryside richer, the campaigns shorter, and the inhabitants friendlier, Napoleon had underestimated the great distances involved and the will of the Russians.

Napoleon met with his generals and staff in a room of the municipal building serving as temporary headquarters. Officer after officer rose to give a somber report on supply lines, condition of matériel, availability of transport horses, general wastage, and troop morale. General after general drew the obvious conclusion that the expedition must stop. Some urged outright turning back; others, because they feared Napoleon's wrath or sensed his wishes, or shared his dream, merely recommended waiting until supplies and conditions improved.

Through it all, Napoleon listened silently. When everyone had had his say, he threw down the pen he had been toying with and said: "All right, then. We still stop the expedition. For now."

Then he rose, circled the room, looked out the window; he moved to a map of Russia and studied it intently.

"No! Cancel that order! We will continue after all!"

He had changed his mind. He launched into a speech, a harangue, really. He lectured his generals, dressed them down, mocked them. His pent-up anger rose as he rambled on. He began to accuse and to insult. It seemed to him inconceivable that the Russians would give up their venerable and treasured cities of Smolensk and Moscow without a fight. The Russians had *their* dignity, even if French generals did not. And once they fought, he would finally have them. He pounded his right fist into the palm of his other hand, as if it were a Russian city. "A single blow delivered at the heart of the Russian Empire, at Moscow the Great, Moscow the Holy, will put this whole blind apathetic mass at my mercy."

So it was on to Smolensk.

While the French generals were trying to stop Napoleon, their Russian counterparts participated in similar stormy scenes at Russian headquarters. General after general rose with reports of the demoralization rife in the French camp. Desertion was rampant, and many deserters, not being French, had no idea why they were in far-off Russia or why they were fighting. Their colleagues, who remained in the ranks only out of fear, would show little inclination, once a battle broke out, to lay down their lives. In the light of this, the vast numerical superiority of the French forces was militarily insignificant. Military considerations aside, this retreat was shaming Russia in the eyes of the world. It tarnished the proud Russian military record. It imperiled the nation. In short, a stand had to be made, and soon.

Kutuzov listened to all this sympathetically. He too wanted to believe all the good news he heard. His intuition, however, told him something else: As long as Napoleon is present in person, you do not start a fight with the Grand Army of France! And suppose the reports turn out to be over-optimistic? The responsibility for the safety of the army, all that stood between Mother Russia and doom, rested heavily on Kutuzov's shoulders.

Kutuzov checked the accuracy of the intelligence information. He doublechecked all the numbers he was given. He made sure of the condition of his own army. The others grew furious at what they took to be simple stalling. They even talked of urging the czar to replace their commander.

Finally Kutuzov retreated in the face of their onslaught. He was a canny old general with a good military record, but he was no charismatic genius like Napoleon. No head of state, he lacked the moral authority and the veto power that the Frenchman had. So the Russian generals were more successful with their commander in chief than the French ones were. The commander who was wrong won the argument, while the commander who was right lost.

Kutuzov backed down and ordered battle positions.

August 16, Smolensk. The long-delayed fight now took place. The French won, but took heavier casualties than the Russians. Napoleon, always better as strategist than a tactician, had left many operations to his generals, who barely cooperated with each other. Afterward, watching the city burn, he thought it "beautiful . . . like Vesuvious erupting."

In the wake of the battle, Napoleon found himself in a charred Smolensk, at the eastern end of a wasted enemy land. As he looked at the scenery, he noticed that some of the leaves were beginning to turn color. Although he possessed more than a hundred thousand fewer troops than he had come with, he still had no decisive victory.

A week passed, during which the pressure again mounted for him to turn back or at least postpone the rest of the campaign until the following year. But, with Moscow only two hundred miles away, Smolensk was the point of no return. To stop now seemed ludicrous. He made the fateful decision, with the nip of autumn already in the air, to press on to Moscow.

Come defeat or victory, going to Moscow was a grand and marvelous feat, while "security" was another word for cowardice, and compromise for the sake of mere survival was petty. He never would have gotten *this* far had he been cautious and reasonable! Only one big battle at Moscow, he kept reminding them, was necessary.

Napoleon's attack force was down now to 160,000 men, but he was lured on by the danger, the casting of the dice, the mirage of a redemptive victory, the daring gamble. It was a romantic dream; he said: "Our very peril urges us on." And he was to say in Moscow, when he felt vindicated: "In politics, you must never retreat, never retrace your steps, never admit a mistake—otherwise, you are discredited. If you have made a mistake, you must persevere—that will put you in the right." So, on August 25, he resumed the advance.

The Russians had lost a battle but hardly the war. The further into Mother Russia the two sides went, the weaker the French army grew through desertions and the stronger the Russian army grew through reenforcements and the growth of paramilitary groups. Nor was Napoleon's morale helped any when on September 2 word came of the French defeat at Salamanca in Spain, at the hands of Wellesley, and of the fall of Madrid.

While the pressure on Napoleon to stop or return continued, so did the pressure on Kutuzov to stop and fight again. Though he preferred not to do battle where he could not be sure of winning, he reluctantly chose Borodino.

September 7. With more and more leaves turning color, another one of the bloodiest battles in history took place between 130,000 Frenchmen (about a fourth of the entering force) and 120,000 Russians. Napoleon, who had a heavy cold that day, behaved listlessly throughout the battle. Many of the instructions he gave were so farfetched that they could not be carried out.

Napoleon's headquarters in the field—his tent, bed, desk, chair.

Late in the battle, Napoleon was in his tent, still feeling feverish and only half aware of the fortunes of the battle. Messengers kept on arriving with urgent requests from officers in the field for the last and best reserves, the Young Guard, to be thrown into action, but to no avail. He worried about being left unprotected deep inside Russia if his premier troops were taken from him. On the other hand, he might be throwing away the one chance he had to finally crush the Russian army, the very chance he had been seeking all these long weeks. After vacillating, he decided to hold them back.

The battle of Borodino, showing little ingenuity on Napoleon's part and costing a quarter of his battle force, was a victory only because the French held the field. The most horrible battle of the Napoleonic Wars, it was, like Eylau, a massacre that crippled both armies equally, with Russian casualties of 58,000 and a French loss of over 30,000. The Russian army had taken a terrible beating at Borodino and lost its position, but it was not destroyed or scattered, it remained a battle force. As in Spain, although the army could not stop the French advance, the will of the people to resist and avenge was stronger than ever.

In the demoralized French camp, with a knockout blow not having been struck at Borodino and with the Grand Army mortally wounded, the generals knew that they could no longer win militarily, whether or not Napoleon accepted the fact.

Now Moscow became even more important, all important, to him. The old Russian capital had lost its military importance but, because of its symbolic value, it still was an important bargaining chip. Napoleon needed it in lieu of a decisive military victory if he was to force the czar to peace terms before winter prevented a retreat.

The same concern—who was to rule Russia?—led Kutuzov to precisely the opposite conclusion, to disregard the symbolism of Moscow. He decided not to defend the capital because Russia's life depended on her having an army in the field; it did not depend on a city, even a key one. So the Russian army abandoned the great city, and the civilian population followed in its wake.

September 14. On a beautiful fall day, with all the leaves turning color, from a hill Napoleon saw the great, glistening, exotic, famous, semioriental cupolas of Moscow.

Grown men, generals—cynics and martinets—wept, hugged, and kissed each other. Even Napoleon, for the first time in ages, looked jovial, childlike, gregarious, contented.

The sight of a lifetime 'for those on this strange journey, it was the climax of one of the most extraordinary adventure stories.

For a glorious while, all thoughts of the miseries and suffering it had taken to get there—the losses, the disappointments, the fading dream, the terrible state of the French army, the bitter arguments, even the hatred—all were erased. Napoleon was ecstatic. There was no telling how many doors were open to him now, how far he could yet go. Although for a while the relentless doubts of the generals had begun to infect even him, he had turned out to be right all along after all. He knew that his destiny would not desert him.

It was a short moment of happiness.

That something was amiss became evident right away. There was one difference between this and all the other capitals he had entered, and it was ominous. Here there was no delegation, as there had always been elsewhere, of obsequious officials to welcome him, no crowd of people to cheer with admiration or to gaze with curiosity or awe at one of the wonders of the world. Moscow was a deserted city, a silent city, a ghost city.

In a letter, he petulantly complained to the czar about the Russians not having left a skeleton administration in Moscow, as had been done in Vienna, Berlin, Madrid. The Russians were not playing fair! He still did not realize that Moscow was not like the other capitals, that the Russians did not consider war to be a game or ritual, and that this campaign was going to be distinctly different from all others.

Napoleon spent an uneasy night in a flea-ridden hovel in the suburbs—an anticlimax to his first sight of Moscow. On the following morning, he rode through empty streets to the ancient palace of the czars, the Kremlin. A day later, he had to flee, with hair and clothing singed, from a fire.

Each side later blamed the other for starting the fire, which raged through the city for almost a week. Many of the houses were made of wood; the fire engines had been removed by the inhabitants; looting and rowdiness was common among the riffraff who had remained behind; some Russian merchants wanted to prevent their goods falling into the hands of the hated enemy; a strong wind was whipping up the flames—all these factors added up to reason enough for a big fire. Whether it had been the result of an accident or of the scorched-earth policy carried to its logical conclusion, the consequences were equally telling: some three-quarters of the city was destroyed. The scene resembled, to Napoleon's eyes, an ocean, a mountain range, a sky, of flames: "The most grand, the most sublime, and the most terrifying sight the world ever beheld!" He even complained in a letter to the czar about the wanton destruction "of one of the most beautiful cities in the world" by this "aimless" scorched-earth policy.

"Aimless"?

Russia had had a capital literally wiped out—but what had Napoleon won? Did he say "aimless"?

A week later, Napoleon returned to the Kremlin and waited. And waited. And waited.

For five weeks he waited. He waited for something to happen. He wrote the czar twice offering to make peace. Alexander, faithful to his vow not to end the fighting until the last intruder left Russian soil, did not even deign to reply. The leaves fell silently.

Napoleon could not understand that if the czar negotiated under the gun, especially after an invasion, he would be deposed or assassinated. He could not understand that, whether because of the new nationalism or old Russian sentimentality, the occupation of Moscow was seen by the Russians as a sacrilege, reenforcing their determination to fight a barbarian invader to the end and if the czar did not follow their resolve, the czar himself would be out of a job. Napoleon did not see the truth of the czar's remark in 1811, "Once the war has begun, one of us must lose his crown."

In desperation, Napoleon toyed with the idea of emancipating and arming the serfs, but that was dangerous and, in any case, irrelevant to a situation in which love of country and hatred of the destructive invader cut across all class lines. He now faced, as he had in Spain, in the Tyrol, and as he soon would in Prussia, something he had not faced before: an enemy who, because of intense popular national feeling, could not be coerced militarily, as the other monarchs regularly used to be, into signing a humiliating peace treaty. The taking of Moscow, like the recent taking of Madrid, instead of bringing the Russians to the peace table—as had the taking of Vienna or Berlin in the good old days of the simpler past—only incited the populace. The five hundred-mile quest for peace negotiations had proved to be an illusion.

Now what? A solemn French staff meeting was held in the very hall of the Kremlin where the czar had declared that he would never negotiate. What should have been a scene of fulfillment and joy over having displaced the Czar was in fact a grim spectacle. There was no movement toward peace on the part of the czar. The reports and proposals Napoleon heard were all equally depressing.

While waiting for a peace offer from the czar that would never come, Napoleon did nothing about the pillaging by his troops. He spent his time dictating letters, taking walks and tours to interesting places in Moscow, or just lying on a sofa and reading novels. A sort of lethargy had overtaken him, as it sometimes does people fortunate enough to reach the Moscow of their dreams. Years later, he realized that he should not have remained so long in Moscow but rather should have gone after the rest of the Russian army. But that was the wisdom—or the delusion—of hindsight.

One of the letters written then consisted of regulations for the famous Comédie Française theater in Paris, regulations good enough to be, for the most part, still on the books today. That was meant to show others, and especially to reassure himself, that everything was normal, that he was still the serene victor and administrator, that wherever Napoleon was was the capital of France, that no aspect of French life escaped his attention and care, and, above all, that absolutely no disaster whatsoever was occupying his thoughts.

Still no response from the czar. More and more, Napoleon was reduced to simply walking in endless circles in his office or bedroom or in the Kremlin's halls, his obese little body stooped, forehead creased, hands folded behind his back, eyes staring vacantly at the ground, ears shut to the world as if listening to some inner voice. He could not even stomach novels anymore. People learned not to interrupt him during such periods of brooding.

Still no response from the czar. Once Moscow was captured, Napoleon had faced three choices: to return to Smolensk for the winter; to try to destroy Kutuzov's army and march north to the czar's capital of St. Petersburg, or to winter in Moscow. The waiting in Moscow reduced the options. As the size and morale of the Russian forces improved and those of the French declined, Napoleon now had a numerically inferior force of about a hundred thousand. That ruled out further advances. To stay in Moscow, so far from Paris, might be no less dangerous, what with all Europe, some prominent Frenchmen included, waiting to take advantage of the first blow to his prestige. There were not, moreover, enough supplies in Moscow to last through the winter. Napoleon therefore had no choice but to consider any plan of departure that would not look like what it in fact was—a retreat.

In the middle of October, ominously on the day after the first snow of the season fell, he finally decided to return to Smolensk and to winter there. He left orders to blow up the Kremlin, but the plan misfired. This uncharacteristic malicious act shows his disillusionment, anger, and despair.

Napoleon at first moved his army south, taking a roundabout way back in order to make the march look like a movement elsewhere rather than a retreat. A week later, a battle occurred with some Russian units barring the way. The French suffered heavy casualties, which they could no longer afford, and Napoleon himself was almost captured by a Cossack band. Given the poor state of his stretched-out supply lines, things looked pretty bad. Winter would merely make the situation worse. Luckily, Kutuzov could not be prevailed upon by the Russian officers to renew the battle.

Because of the many weeks wasted in Vilna, Vitebsk, and Moscow on the way in, the return trip was undertaken a month too late into the autumn. It began well enough, although the army was slowed down by the heavy load of useless plunder the soldiers were dragging along. The countryside was devastated, and provisions that had been brought from Moscow soon ran out. Men dropped by the wayside from hunger or weariness. Russian prisoners of war had to be shot. The French wounded were left behind, only to be butchered by angry peasants, guerrillas, or Cossack horsemen. All the horrors of the marches in the broiling sun of Egypt and Syria and in the snow and ice of Spain were being repeated, and outdone, in this Russian nightmare.

Napoleon showed no more of his famous foresight in the retreat than he had in the advance on Moscow. He did not coordinate movements with the French forces in adjacent areas;

A scene during the retreat from Moscow. A contemporary lithograph.

he did not give up a pointless siege of Riga. He knew little about the Russian winter and never tried to find out. He did nothing to prepare his troops for cold weather. He even neglected to have the horses specially shod for the winter ice and snow.

Kutuzov meanwhile dogged the French but prudently kept his distance from them. He was content to let nature and disintegration and guerrilla warfare and hunger do the work for him rather than risk a defeat or even another Borodino.

November 6. Napoleon heard that one of his subsidiary forces had suffered a defeat and that in Paris, a deranged general, claiming that the emperor was dead, almost succeeded in setting up a provisional government. This was exactly what Napoleon had feared. If the general had not been clearly a lunatic but a shrewd politician, would the attempt still have failed? That close call awakened in Napoleon all his chronic insecurities about being on top. How fragile his hold on power was despite all his military victories, diplomatic wheeling-dealing, and imperial splendor! Did he recall now the most famous sentence the greatest French essayist, Montagne, had written two hundred years earlier: "Upon the most exalted throne in the world, we are still sitting only on our own rump"?

Although the crown was supposed to go to his son and heir, as it would have in a traditional monarchy, the incident revealed that he was still only an upstart and that what was written in the glossy new lawbooks under his close supervision meant little. The fabric of his government would come apart like so much rotted wool if it were not for the magic of one name. And now in Russia that name was stuck in mud and facing disaster. On the next day, very cold weather began. Then came snow again. Then came lots more snow.

The army eagerly looked forward to food, rest, matériel, and winter quarters in Smolensk. When they finally reached that city, however, they found only disappointment. The distribution system had broken down completely, and Smolensk was as charred as Moscow, worse even. More snow fell. Napoleon wasted additional time before leaving Smolensk, thereby giving Kutuzov a chance to seize thirty-five thousand prisoners, mainly stragglers.

November 22. Napoleon heard, while watching the snowflakes swirl around him silently, that Minsk, his next supply depot, had been captured by the Russians. Two days later came word that his bridge over the Berezina River had been destroyed.

As if things were not horrible enough, Mother Nature now joined in the tormenting. The cold weather caused far more deaths in a short time than had the hunger and continual harrassment by guerrilla and Cossack bands. Because many horses froze to death, within a week what was left of the once glorious Grand Army was bereft of cavalry, artillery, and supplies.

November 28–9. The horrors reached a climax when a mob of twenty-five thousand soldiers from the main force and forty thousand noncombatants reached the Berezina River. Enemy troops blocked various access routes. A bridge had to be built quickly by men standing chest-deep in freezing water while the Russian forces converged. After a minor battle, the main force got across. Then the bridge was deliberately destroyed by the French, leaving behind some thirty thousand individuals— stragglers,. wounded soldiers, noncombatants, women and children—to die of cold, hunger, thick snow, Cossack lancers, and gunfire from Russian regulars. It was a scene that would make Dante's *Inferno* look like a vacation resort. A few days later, the December temperature fell to below zero. Entire portions of the remaining army simply disappeared.

What had occurred was without parallel in modern history. The greatest general and ruler of the time, perhaps of all time, after having, with a huge half-million man army, invaded a country, occupied its capital, and not lost a single battle, was forced to begin a retreat during which his army simply dissolved. What had begun as an apparent maneuver soon had turned into a retreat and, finally, into a rout. Did Alexander, Czar of All the Russias and the Lord's Anointed, remember at this time the humiliating aftermath to that awful defeat at Austerlitz years earlier? Now the shoe was at long last on the other foot. If Napoleon were the type, it would have been his turn to sit down by the side of the road and weep like a child. If he could have found a place to sit in the snow.

The statistics on the expedition were staggering. While the Russians lost the huge number of two hundred thousand soldiers, French losses far exceeded this. Of the half million or so who entered Russia, bands barely adding up to a few thousand eventually returnied. Napoleon frankly admitted in his famous Bulletin Number 29—issued just before he left the army—the defeat and dissolution of the Grand Army. He blamed it on nature and God. Such an unprecedented loss might well seem like an act of divine vengeance to those who read history from a religious standpoint.

The fault, however, was mainly Napoleon's own. Although one of the French generals echoed Napoleon's excuse when he said, "General Famine and General Winter, rather than the Russian bullets, have conquered the Grand Army," the catastrophe was mainly caused by failure to anticipate obstacles and to establish effective supply lines that took into account the Russian landscape. Such a failure was not due to a falling off in Napoleon's intellectual powers but to overconfidence, to the belief in his special destiny, to the consequent inability to listen to advice. For instance, he had shrugged off warnings about the unique size of Russia with the glib remark, "And as for hugeness, it merely means that many more victorious marches."

Besides the major error of not settling with Spain one way or the other before starting for Moscow and thus depriving himself of some of his best French troops, Napoleon was also undone by his own thoroughness, of all things. In one of the greatest ironies of all, the vast numerical superiority that he brought with him paradoxically helped the Russians and hurt the French because it forced the Russians to retreat rather than fight. His taking no chances inadvertently made the Russians take no chances and made them lure the French to their destruction deep inside Russia, to be swallowed by the Russian land and climate. As Napoleon said afterward, in words that only partly apply to this situation: "The mistakes of our enemies often are more useful to them than their abilities and cause us to commit mistakes still greater than theirs." With a smaller, leaner army of better quality and greater mobility, Napoleon would have been able to tempt the Russians into an early battle, and, because of his by now legendary strategic sense, he might well have then defeated them as he had on various occasions in 1805–7.

Thoughts about the past or about what might have been, however, appear not to have been on Napoleon's mind during the retreat. He seemed unaware of the disaster, indifferent to the fate of the army left behind, remorseless about the sufferings and death of so many of his own men. Throughout the campaign, in fact, he (and his Guard) had had the best food and shelter. Bulletin Number 29 concluded by reassuring everyone that "His Majesty's health has never been better." (And why should it not have been, considering that he had not partaken of the agony of his soldiers?) He, the center of the universe, was still in charge of France, and despite exaggerated rumors of his death and despite an abortive coup, he would be back in Paris soon enough.

No, not Moscow or the past preoccupied Napoleon but Paris and the future. During the retreat, he worried about the reactions of the governments and peoples of Europe to his tremendous losses, as well as to the conspiracy in Paris. He felt the need to be in his capital when, or before, the bad news spread. He feared, frankly, for his throne and his life.

He himself was France. He alone could hold the regime together, unite the classes, keep the people in line, raise armies, browbeat his allies into loyalty, defeat the enemy on the battlefield or at the negotiating table. Above all, new armies had to be raised quickly, for all his power and his marvels stemmed from the martial drumbeat.

So, on December 5, accompanied by his counsellors and servants, he left the Grand Army (such as it was), raced across Europe, and, two weeks later, rushed into the Tuileries palace in Paris. To many, it looked like desertion, the abandonment of an army that was foundering, as he had shown himself capable of doing in Egypt in 1799, and, in a way, in Spain in 1809.

In the meantime, his army, now only packs of wild men, reached their last hope, Vilna. Finding there, and then in Kovno, only more unexpected suffering, they plundered everyone and everything.

So ended the greatest campaign in modern history.

In early 1812, Napoleon had told someone that he was beginning "the greatest and most difficult enterprise that I have so far attempted." And indeed the capture of Moscow was, at first, the last of the series of climaxes that had begun exactly a decade earlier with the *Te Deum* celebrated in Notre Dame on the occasion of the Peace of Amiens and the Concordat with the Church. He felt sure that a century later everyone, seeing then the wisdom of his having tried to prevent the overrunning of Europe by "those barbarians of the north," would say "Napoleon was right." This consoled him for his fiasco. As did also his remark, years later on St. Helena, that, had he died in the Kremlin, at the zenith of his career, "I should have had the greatest glory, the greatest reputation that has ever existed. . . . If I had succeeded, I should have been the greatest man known to history."

If. . . .

CHAPTER TEN

Closing the Ring

(1 8 1 3 – 1 8 1 4)

The capture of Moscow, some 1,400 miles from Paris, was the furthest reach of the French Empire—and of the Napoleonic dream. It capped sixteen years of victories and conquests. After that, the road was downhill most of the way. Although Napoleon was to win some of his most brilliant battles in the next year and a half, he was no longer fighting wars of advance and conquest but of retreat and defense. In a sense, the retreat of the French army which began at Moscow did not really end, despite some stops and brief comebacks at various way stations in Germany and France, until it reached Paris itself.

The invasion of Russia had been the high point of a policy followed for a decade and a half—victory in the field to be followed by diplomacy and political demands. The long series of successful conquests convinced Napoleon that his policy could not fail. Moscow, therefore, came as a shock, from which he emerged a divided man. On the one hand, he was run-down physically and psychologically. He tired easily; his mind sometimes seemed less clear; he blamed others more than ever when things went wrong. On the other hand, he still believed in his star. Even the abandonment and loss of a large army followed by a return to Paris could be the prelude to great deeds—as had happened after Aboukir Bay and the abandonment of the army in Egypt.

So the disaster in Russia was not, as might be expected, followed by the collapse of Napoleon's empire. On the contrary, it took almost a year and a half and the effort of all Europe to bring him to unconditional surrender. The momentum of French and Napoleonic prestige and power was hard to slow down and stop. He had after all defeated the Russian army and captured their capital. In every war for sixteen years, the French might have lost battles but never the war. Nor would he face in Europe such supply problems as had so seriously undermined his victories in Russia.

On returning home to the Tuileries (December 18, 1812), Napoleon was cheerful. He seemed unaware that his world power was broken. He might have lost a big army in Russia, but he had a second big army in Spain and numerous garrisons all over Europe. He was sure that he could soon build up a new military force to destroy Russia. A Prussian declaration of war against France made it easier for him to appeal to his nation to help him raise forces. And this time, unlike in 1812, most of the soldiers—reaching the vast figure of one million—were French. Although the army was not the equal of some earlier ones, its leaders were veterans. Their faith in Napoleon, shaken for a while, was not yet permanently impaired, and he knew how to render them eager to make up for the rout in Russia. So Napoleon looked forward to resuming the war. The financial problems he faced were also overcome; he seized the funds of the local governments in return for paper certificates. His personal wealth he left untouched.

Now came a desperate and grand phase in Napoleon's life. He took charge of affairs again with ruthlessness and zeal. He spent the four months between his return from Russia and a new campaign against Prussia working at his normal frenzied pace. First, by great striving and in the midst of all the other business of running a large empire, he was able to put together an army of 225,000 in Germany, right after the Russian campaign and losses. Then he rushed off to supervise complex field operations against large forces. Defeat and collapse hardly seemed imminent. He was so certain of destroying a new Russo-Prussian alliance and regaining European supremacy that, even in the wake of the loss of his Grand Army in Russia, he still neglected to make peace with Spain. Had he done so, he could have brought his fine army there into Germany, where it would have made a difference.

Napoleon was unaware that throughout Europe the spirit of the French Revolution was rising. People wanted to be liberated, not from old regimes but from militarism, state control, and French domination. Nowhere was this more the case than in Prussia. In dealing with local resistance there, Napoleon was severe, ordering the taking of hostages and the shooting of every tenth person. Such ruthlessness merely laid the groundwork for a more intense reaction and for the national resentment that soon flowered.

Prussia was the first state to take advantage of Napoleon's slipping. In the retreat from Moscow, the Prussian contingent became separated from the main French army, and the Prussian general signed an agreement allowing the Russians passage through East Prussia. This signaled a change in Prussia's affiliation. The same Prussia passively overrun by the French in 1806–7 now was aroused. Ready for a fight to the finish, it fielded a large army in a burst of nationalism and pride.

Kutuzov had been content merely to oust the French from Russia. He was overruled by the czar, who held that they should be driven across the Rhine and into their own land. It became clear that this could be done and peace finally obtained only if Prussia, Austria, and Russia joined forces in a new coalition. In the spring of 1813, Prussia entered into an open alliance with the czar and declared war on France. The Russian army entered Prussia, joined forces with the newly active Prussians, and headed toward France.

The allies at first merely wanted Napoleon humiliated and cut down to size, not destroyed or dethroned. Given his enemies' war weariness, their fear of popular revolutionary movements, and their rivalry among themselves for territorial possessions, Napoleon could have dealt with the new coalition by means of diplomacy and compromises, as Talleyrand was to do in January 1815. For instance, the Austrians (who were to join the alliance a little later) were, as late as February 1814, interested in the Bonapartist-Hapsburg dynasty in France and were suspicious of the goals of the Russians and the Prussians. Napoleon in the past excelled at negotiating separately with great powers in order to exploit their rivalries. But such negotiations at this juncture for France meant that Napoleon would have to renounce the Grand Empire and the Confederation of the Rhine; he would have to accept a European balance of power in which France was merely one among equals. Such a return to France's natural frontiers, something he would gladly settle for later and which was acceptable now to everyone else, seemed to him an abject surrender, a downright humiliation.

However high his credentials as a diplomat, peacemaker, administrator, and lawmaker might be, in his own eyes his prestige and glory rested mainly on his military achievements. To give up his conquests and return to the borders of 1795 would call into question his reign, his greatness, his very identity. That in turn would lead either to his being toppled or to his remaining in office with greatly reduced powers. The

French, deprived of glory abroad, would insist now on having liberty at home instead, with all its inconvenience for him.

A dynastic ruler could lose much territory (as did the Emperor Francis) without having to answer for it. Napoleon felt himself to be in a different situation. He had taken over a country already expanded beyond its traditional frontiers, and he had extended those borders and subjected most of the continent. If he gave up any of this territory, he felt, rightly or wrongly, that he would be called to account. He feared that, unlike a legitimate, hereditary king, he himself, "who rose to power through the [military] camp," could be undone by one setback, one sign of weakness, one stroke of bad luck. To all who beseeched him now to seize the opportunity for peace—diplomats, ambassadors, generals, politicians, committees—he, the great man at bay, had one set speech, one recurring cluster of ideas:

As soon as I cease to be feared, my Empire is destroyed. What would be an indifferent matter to a king of an old dynasty is very serious to me. Among the anciently established sovereigns, war aims never go beyond possessions of a province or a fortress. With me, the stake is always my existence and that of the whole Empire.

In France, he felt, everybody thought they had helped Napoleon to power and was owed something. If Napoleon lost, they would all desert him. Both at home and abroad, therefore, he had to rule by fear. His power depended on his glory, and his glory depended on his victories. "Conquest made me what I am; conquest alone can keep me there."

So the only alternative seemed to Napoleon—if to no one else in France—to be, as ever, rapid and decisive military action, and more dubious ordeals for the French people.

In April 1813, Napoleon left Paris and marched to Leipzig with 140,000 men. Three allied armies were approaching from north, east, and south. At Leipzig, he waited, as was his habit, for one of them to make an error. Within a few weeks, he struck and won a big victory at Lützen, though at a high price. The enemy, with inferior forces, fought well. Then came another quick victory at Bautzen, again with heavy casualties on both sides. Considering that the superior French forces, led by the greatest of commanders, faced a weaker force with a disunited command, the results were disappointing. The battles of Lützen and Bautzen were empty victories because he did not gain a decisive advantage from them. The war weariness of the French officers and veterans may have been a factor, but the main reason had to do with a by-product of the Russian campaign. The huge loss of eighty thousand horses in Russia could not be made up quickly, leaving him with a cavalry too weak for pursuit of the routed foe.

Both sides had expected to beat the other quickly, and now they found themselves at a stalemate. Napoleon, having to give up hope of an immediate, definitive military victory, resorted to his other forte, diplomacy. He surprised everyone by calling for an armistice. This is now generally regarded as a serious error. He himself knew that it halted his momentum, but he was worried about the cavalry problem and by Austria's intentions. The interlude, which he used to resupply himself with four hundred thousand men and matériel, also gave the battered allies a breathing space.

Then, in the midst of the peace negotiations came word that at Vitoria in Spain, Wellesley (Wellington) with eighty thousand troops defeated a French force of sixty-five thousand (June 1813). Their retreat cut off, the French had to abandon all their matériel and all the art treasures taken from Madrid. The Spanish campaign was still, as in 1812, a hemorrhaging of Napoleon's power.

The peace conference now adjourned as Austria decided to declare war on France for the third time in eight years. Soon Britain joined the allies to form the Fourth Coalition. The

Austrian army and British gold, neutralizing Russian and Prussian desires for undue revenge and compensation, would work for a balance of power in Europe.

When fighting resumed, therefore, Napoleon faced nothing less than a united Europe and a situation far more favorable to his enemies. The allies had 800,000 men to Napoleon's 470,000, with many of the latter being raw new conscripts. Three allied armies adopted Napoleon's own strategy of defeating the enemy piecemeal. They would attack only those of his forces led by his generals. Because of his military genius and because he kept the best troops for himself, they would delay risking a battle with him until they had worn his army down by attrition.

Napoleon decided to establish his headquarters at Dresden, the capital of Saxony and center of his defense of the Elbe River. While he was out on operations in the field, one allied force, the Army of Bohemia, made a surprise attack on Dresden. Napoleon marched his forces back to Dresden, covering ninety miles in seventy-two hours. In the large battle that ensued, the French won brilliantly. One hundred fifty thousand soldiers were thrown back by half that number. Then a rainstorm came up and a very tired Napoleon, sleepless for four days and nights, did not track down the fleeing enemy force in person. The pursuing French commanders, without their leader's presence, acted with great carelessness. In his prime, Napoleon would have destroyed the defeated foe. Instead, what might have been one of his greatest victories, ended up being a stage in a losing campaign. The French now suffered a series of defeats that cost Napoleon a hundred thousand men and reversed, within a few days after Dresden, what had looked like a quick, victorious end to the campaign. Because of desertion, sickness, and poor supply lines, in addition to the outright defeats, the French army was in a short time cut down to 250,000 men from 400,000. Napoleon marched and countermarched around Dresden, exhausting his men in trying to bring about a definitive engagement. Indecisiveness had overtaken him, and he dawdled in Dresden while his position there grew untenable.

Finally in October, he moved his forces to Leipzig for a better position or, as it might be, a last stand. There he faced an allied force of two hundred fifty thousand. A three-day battle ensued, the climatic Battle of the Nations, which was watched from a nearby hill by the czar and the king of Prussia. The first day was inconclusive, but luck was leaving the French. Napoleon was running short of ammunition. More important, his timing was off. Beginning with 190,000 men against 200,000, he had an excellent chance of winning. Ignoring news that enemy reenforcements were on the way, however, he started the battle too late.

Even when the possibility of defeat was clear at the end of the first day and he could have got his army away safely, Napoleon did not order a retirement from Leipzig. He had decided to stake everything on one more try. On the second day the allies attacked with a force now grown to three hundred thousand and, after long, bitter struggle, they captured the main French position. When Napoleon finally ordered the retirement, there was great confusion. The next day, the allies attacked and forced the French into the inner city, where the streets and gates were hopelessly crowded with retreating soldiers. A bridge was blown up by the French soldiers too soon and, as at the Berezina River, a large part of the French army was left stranded.

Soon thereafter, in the central square of Leipzig, where chaos had reigned a short while before, Czar Alexander and King Frederick William, with their generals—later joined by Emperor Francis—celebrated the great victory. The French lost a huge seventy thousand men, the Allies fifty-four thousand, a decisive, even staggering, defeat. Leipzig, like the entire campaign of 1813 of which it was the climax, confirmed the trend established by the retreat from Moscow and indicated the end of Napoleon's rise to power.

At least that was the way Europe saw it. As the badly wounded French army retreated to the Rhine, Bavaria switched sides from France to the allies. Soon the many princes of the Confederation of the Rhine did likewise. Holland and Naples erupted in rebellion. Overnight the empire was ablaze and tottering. The Spanish campaign, as usual, was going from bad to worse. The French themselves were sick of war. The destiny of France was clearly no longer the same as, or parallel to, that of Napoleon. On November 9, 1813, Napoleon reentered Paris, having, for the second time in a year, abandoned a huge territory and lost an army of half a million men.

In their December 1813 sessions, the French legislatures, under Napoleon usually docile collections of "yes-men," called on the emperor to accept peace terms and demanded civil and political liberties. Napoleon at once dissolved the legislatures, saying that he, not they, represented the nation. Yet he himself realized that the spirit of 1793 was gone. War weariness and despotism had lowered the morale of the French people.

The allies could invade France itself now with huge forces, but they hesitated. They were also war weary, and a fight in France would be terribly bloody. So they tried negotiations. They were still willing in late 1813 to let Napoleon keep his throne, as well as to recognize the "natural" frontiers of France and the French conquest of the Low Countries (both having been achieved by the zealous armies of Revolutionary France in 1793). The offer was perhaps meant to turn the French people against their leader. Napoleon was still firmly in charge, however, and he hoped for a military solution or a miracle. He would not give up his personal dream or, he thought, leave France weaker than he had found her. His swollen ego was now hopelessly confusing issues, so that he could not disentangle the interests of France from his own.

But then, with Holland liberated from France and Britain fearful that the great port of Antwerp in French hands would be a threat to British security, the allied negotiators pushed instead for the "ancient," pre-Revolutionary frontiers. The French representative to a peace conference, seeing few options open to a defeated France, agreed to the change. Napoleon overruled him. Insisting, in a half-hearted peace gesture, on the word "natural," he said privately that "ancient" would mean a French capitulation and the resumption of war by him within two years. The peace conference—unlike the many in which a victorious and dominating Napoleon participated—therefore broke down. Having dictated to Europe for over a decade, he was not used to being dictated to. He turned again to the military option. He would either win back Europe or fight to the bitter end.

This inflexibility undid him, for even after France was invaded and losing he still could have kept the throne at the price of a return to the old French frontiers. Was he waging a heroic defense on behalf of France, or was he blocked by an egotistic inability to admit defeat and to participate in compromise? Probably he himself did not know.

While talking peace, he had been making feverish military preparations. He had raised for the second time in a year an entirely new army. Speeding up military conscription, he wanted to induct nearly half a million new men. He could, however, put only 150,000 men in the field because of draft dodging and equipment shortages. The situation was far worse at the end of 1813 than at the beginning of the year. The losses of the recent campaign in Germany affected him more than had those of the Russian campaign. The army he had taken to Russia was only partly French, whereas the one in Germany was almost entirely French.

The combined losses of the past two years, moreover, were so enormous they created great discontent among the people and even among his officers. Morale was as low as it had been just before Napoleon had seized power. In the bitter winter of 1813–14, the French were sick of a quarter-century of war, of taxes and deficits, of labor shortages and economic dislocations caused by the closing of foreign markets. Wanting no part of a now-hopeless struggle, they dodged conscription and taxes. And, although his veterans used to be ready to lay down their lives for him with a religious fervor, it must have become clear by now to many that he was hardly a perfect general. By one computation, he lost six out of twelve campaigns. The administrative departments of his army were lamely run. His own soldiers were fed and paid very badly. They were poorly armed, and the medical facilities were awful. No longer seeming invincible, he began to seem downright unlucky, as a typhus epidemic carried off another hundred thousand soldiers at this critical juncture. Money was short, and he even had to withdraw funds at last from his immense private fortune stashed away in the Tuileries basement, something he refused to do until then.

At this bitter time, he did what he should have done years before, rid himself of two of his worst mistakes: the fight with the pope and the Spanish misadventure. He released the pope and recognized one of the Bourbons as king of Spain after all. But his actions came too late for them to do him much good.

If 1813 saw the battle for Germany, 1814 saw the battle for France itself. The allies, operating with over a million soldiers, decided to send 350,000 of them across the Rhine. In early 1814, the Austrian army passed through Switzerland into France. A Prussian army soon crossed the Rhine further north. Napoleon placed his new, poorly prepared troops in the field. Hoping to take on one enemy army at a time, he went on the offensive. At the battle of La Rothière, he lost to a far superior foe and found himself in a hopeless situation. Two armies, each bigger than his own, were marching to Paris. Belgium had fallen in the north, and the enemy was advancing in the south of France as well.

A rift in the allied camp developed suddenly. The Russians and the Prussians wanted to take Paris and dethrone

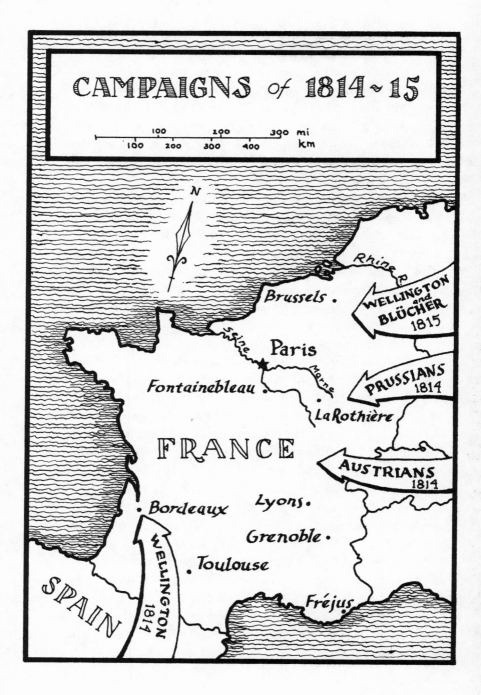

Napoleon. The Austrians, worried as much about Russian as French ascendancy, were still content, along with Britain, to leave Napoleon on the throne.

The allied troops were poorly coordinated, and Napoleon won a series of quick victories. His defensive campaign along the Marne and Seine rivers in France in the winter of 1814 is a textbook example of how a small force, brilliantly led by one determined man of great experience and talent and fighting on excellent interior (short) lines of communications and supply, can wreak havoc on a far larger force spread out over a wide area and led by a divided, often squabbling, command. It was Napoleon at his finest as a general. This campaign, fought with Napoleon's back to the wall, was as brilliant as the one of 1796 in Italy, with which he had begun his career as general-diplomat. It was more brilliant even, considering that now he fought with an inferiority of one to four. Even after the traumatic loss of the Grand Army in Russia, Napoleon had had greater military resources than he did now in 1814. Yet without depression or weariness, he worked around the clock and inspired everyone. This war of heroic defiance was superb drama: the legendary warrior at bay, fighting off the whole world, going down swinging. Yet it was also futile, wasteful, insane. It certified that he would have to be removed from power—if he survived at all.

In February 1814, Napoleon attacked Prussian forces along the Marne and gave them a severe drubbing. In the meantime the main allied army crossed the Seine and advanced to Paris. Napoleon still thought that his star was rising and that the people supported him against foreign invaders. He dashed back to the Seine and beat another army. A few days later, urging activism on one of his generals, he claimed that with a core of less than six thousand elite troops, he had destroyed three armies and taken forty thousand prisoners, "and thrice saved the capital." Even after making allowances for exaggeration, one has to concede that in this campaign he came as close to being a superman as anyone ever did.

*The lion at bay: Napoleon during the grim Battle of France in 1814.
One of the most famous of all paintings of him, it is not by a contemporary
witness, but an imaginative reconstruction a half century later.*

Yet it was all in vain. His victories slowed down the
enemy, but they could not affect the drift of the campaign, could
not stem the tide of Europe. He was being worn down by sheer
numbers converging on him from every direction. Even in the
south, where things moved slowly, Wellesley, now the Duke of
Wellington, won a battle, captured the large southern French

city of Bordeaux, and raised the royalist flag. On March 14, the four great powers (Russia, Austria, Prussia, and Britain) pledged to continue the war for twenty years if need be and to rule out the possibility of a separate peace on the part of any member. How much longer could Napoleon hold out?

His strategy now was to harass the flanks and rear of the allied army marching on Paris. Ordering that Paris be turned into a fortress, he wanted to fight his last battle, like the legendary Hector, in front of the capital. The Parisians, however, refused to join his army or prepare for the invaders. Napoleon's brother Joseph, who had been placed in charge of the defense of the capital itself, was weak and incompetent. Talleyrand was acting treacherously behind the emperor's back. As he had predicted would happen in adversity, Napoleon was being abandoned on all sides. He was isolated as an adventurer in his own empire and capital.

On hearing of the despair, panic, and treachery sweeping Paris, the allied forces made directly for the city. On March 29, they began the attack, and the next day the unprepared city surrendered. The allies having had three days' advance on Napoleon, Paris fell before he could return and see to the defense in person.

Napoleon was finished.

On March 31, 1814, an enemy army marched into Paris for the first time in almost four hundred years. The czar and the king of Prussia entered the city with them, saw the sights, and celebrated the triumphant end of a bitter, decade-long struggle.

On a main road to Paris, a grim-faced Napoleon, at the head of a small entourage—much smaller than usual—rode at a gallop. Suddenly a courier came from the opposite direction and signaled a desire to speak to them. Napoleon ignored him, but one of the generals took the message. He raced ahead and caught up with the emperor. "Sire, Paris has fallen!"

Leaving his troops, Napoleon hastened ahead by himself. Although talking of peace, he was still not ready to give up. He finally went to the castle of Fontainebleau, the very place where the pope had been interned until just a short time ago.

Under allied direction, the Senate deposed Napoleon on April 2 and elected a provisional government of five members, headed by Talleyrand. Talleyrand was to work out the details of a new constitution. The allies also had an easy time detaching the generals from their former emperor. His once loyal marshals were exhausted from so much fighting, disillusioned with the cause, and eager now only to save the titles and the wealth they had amassed.

The advice the generals gave Napoleon was therefore the same as the allies had insisted on, the Senate legislated, and popular opinion favored: abdication in favor of his son. Napoleon took time considering the idea. But by then the czar, influenced by Talleyrand, demanded unconditional surrender. The announcement made by the allies occupying Paris indicated they refused to deal with Napoleon's family but would recognize the integrity of pre-Revolutionary France. Once again, Napoleon, by waiting too long and reaching for the impossible, had forfeited a compromise that would have left him something substantial. His belated abdication in favor of his son was now spurned.

The cornered Napoleon wanted to raise an army of sixty thousand and march with it to Paris. In a dramatic showdown at Fontainebleau on April 4, the generals warned him against turning Paris into another Moscow. Napoleon was determined. When they continued to oppose him, he sternly announced that he would do without them and lead the army himself.

One of his top generals pointed out that the army would refuse to march.

But Napoleon felt the army would obey him.

"The army will obey its leaders," the general calmly responded.

Napoleon signs the Act of Abdication at Fontainbleau, 6 April 1814.

Napoleon stared, clenched his fist and teeth, then shrugged his shoulders and shook his head. He realized that it was true.

On April 6 he abdicated unconditionally.

On the same day that Napoleon signed the deed of abdication, the Senate accepted the new constitution and made the unpopular Count of Provence, brother of the executed Louis XVI, king of France with the title of Louis XVIII. On April 11, the four allies signed a peace treaty with France which ruled out any claim Napoleon might have to the throne. After a long hesitation, he added his name to the document on the next day, signing away power he no longer possessed.

Did he remember at this juncture the czar's warning of a few years before, the prophetic words, "Once the war has begun, one of us must lose his crown"?

That same night, he tried, unsuccessfully, to poison himself.

CHAPTER ELEVEN

Elba, the Hundred Days, Waterloo

(1814–1815)

The abdication of April 6, 1814 was the real end of Napoleon's career. What followed was a long coda, sunset, or anticlimax, the messiness caused when a great man cannot read the exit cues being given him by history and insists on making a fool of himself onstage.

Instead of being imprisoned or facing a firing squad, Napoleon was treated mildly by the allies because of the intercession of the czar and because he had not done anything that had not been done, if more ineptly, by some legitimate ruler (for instance, Louis XIV or Frederick the Great of Prussia) in the past. Yet he had to be deposed because his irrepressible personality threatened the peace of Europe. Ironically, when he himself had deposed the rulers in Italy, Germany, and Spain, the historical idea of the divine right of kings had been undermined forever.

The allies' Treaty of Fontainebleau (April 1814) left Napoleon, in return for the surrender by the Bonaparte family of all their titles and claims, the title of emperor and gave him the island of Elba as his realm. This deference to Napoleon's megalomania was either high generosity or mischievous mockery. He was allowed an income of two million francs a year and a force of four hundred of his guardsmen.

At first, Napoleon delayed leaving because he could not believe that the end had finally come. Some miracle might restore him yet. At last, on April 20, in a famous scene at the palace of Fontainebleau, he took a tearful leave of the guard, which had been with him at many of his great victories. He was distressed to find that almost everyone had deserted him in his dark hour. Even his wife, Princess Marie Louise, rather than insisting on sharing her husband's fate, allowed herself and her son to be put in Austrian hands. Napoleon was too proud and ashamed to ask her to join him.

As Napoleon's coach and convoy made its way to the Mediterranean coast, crowds formed in various towns along the way. After trying in vain to block the coaches, they stood at the sides of the road, jeering, cursing, and throwing stones. In one place, Napoleon was hanged in effigy. The man before whom all Europe had recently trembled became panic-stricken. To the surprise of the allied commissioners traveling with him, he was so cowardly as to disguise himself as an Austrian courier in order to save his life.

In some ways, Napoleon's journey was a return to his roots. The point of departure from France was the very harbor town of Fréjus where he had landed fifteen years earlier on his return from Egypt to begin his meteoric political career. Having originally come from a Mediterranean island, he now returned to one, one in fact within sight of his native Corsica. Ever the dreamer, even at this terrible hour, he believed that his story was not over. "I shall always be an extraordinary man," he humbly declared.

Elba was small, with a population at that time of about ten thousand. As if the island were a great empire and he would remain there for good, Napoleon established, out of sheer habit or vanity, a miniature machinery of government, complete with a court, a budget, and a standing army of three thousand men (though it soon dwindled to half that amount). The bulk of his expenses went for his "army," his "navy," and his "imperial residences." All this make-believe fed his hunger for activity and public display. It may also have been a cover-up for any more serious plans he might be considering.

His mother visited him there, as did a sister and a mistress. So did tourists, who generally found that his appearance did not suggest anything of his reputed greatness, at least not until he began to speak. A fat, chatty, amiable little man, he seemed more like a priest or friar than a hero.

After a few months, he lost interest in his Lilliputian empire—or began seriously to plan a comeback. Even if he had not thought of one from the beginning, he had good reason to do so now. The French government reneged on its promised annual grant of money to him. He heard rumors that some allied leaders wanted him deported to a remote island or that he might be assassinated. If he was surrounded by allied spies, he in turn was kept aware of developments on the continent by agents of his own. He learned from them that people in France were eager for his return, and many in Italy hoped that he would take over their country.

Even his mother urged him to fulfill his destiny, which was surely not to die on Elba. A self-made emperor with unique experience had been suddenly deprived of his power and publicity. Bored and frustrated, he was at forty-six as ambitious as any young lieutenant. With him still at the height of his mental and physical powers, who could believe that his career was over and that the luck of this energetic man had run out? Napoleon himself later said that what made him return was the thought of being accused of cowardice and of fear of death.

The occasion, or excuse, for his return must have been the news from France, where people had much to complain about. At the time of Napoleon's fall, Talleyrand had advised the allies that France would never tolerate another Bonaparte regime or a king imposed by outsiders and that their only option therefore was to recall the legitimate heirs to the throne, the Bourbons. When Louis XVIII entered Paris, he was cheered by an enthusiastic crowd, although only a small portion of the populace had wanted the restoration of the Bourbons.

The cheering soon stopped. Louis was not a malevolent person, but his blind insistence on the divine right of kings, after all that had happened in the past quarter of a century, showed him to be out of touch with reality. Under him, the royalists returned to France and reclaimed their former property. The government's reopening of the Revolutionary land settlement alarmed the middle class and the peasants. Veterans were dismissed or put on half pay. The worst of the wartime taxes were retained despite the arrival of peace. The government, conducted by royalist politicians, made numerous other mistakes of judgment and tact. With almost every deed, the restored Bourbons further alienated the army and the population. They made the already somewhat mythical Napoleon shine out as a hero of the Revolution. As someone (perhaps Napoleon himself) memorably said at this time, the Bourbons had "learned nothing and forgotten nothing." They "reopened everything which had been settled" by revolution and empire.

Ironically, while he was in practice less liberal than Louis XVIII, Napoleon, with his excellent sense of public relations, propaganda, self-advertisement, and image projection, stood for the principles of 1789, and the dull Louis stood for a benighted past. With the foreign troops removed from Paris, the restored Bourbon government, hollow at the core, clearly would collapse at a push. Napoleon might well have remembered what happened to the disreputable Directory on his return from Egypt in 1799.

When should Napoleon make his move? After the collapse of France, the allied governments had gathered at the Congress of Vienna to reorganize the continent on a conservative basis. Tensions grew to such an extent that for a while it seemed as if Austria, Britain, and France would go to war against Russia and Prussia. Such discord among the allies was music to Napoleon's ears. On hearing (erroneously, it turned out) that the Congress had adjourned, he thought that his opportunity had come.

On the first of March 1815, he landed in southern France at the head of his army of twelve hundred men. The Congress was in fact still in session when the shattering news came a few days later that Napoleon had left Elba and was proceeding to Paris. Fortunately for the conferees, here was one topic they all agreed on and could act on at once in concert. In less than an hour, they decided on war. Within a week, declaring Napoleon the enemy of world peace and an outlaw, they reconstituted the Fourth Coalition against France and prepared to redo the work of 1814.

Historians have outdone each other in using superlatives to describe Napoleon's reconquest of his empire in a mere 18 days' march to Paris with only a handful of troops and without a shot fired. It is a fairy tale, one of the most remarkable events in all history, the most wonderful and exhilarating of romantic adventures, the most melodramatic part of a career filled with incredible happenings and achievements, the most spectacular episode in Napoleon's amazing life. Later he himself more modestly called the march from Cannes to Paris "the happiest period in my life."

With his understanding of the French people, Napoleon realized that the middle class, tired of his despotism and his taxing wars, were not too eager for his return but that the

common people and peasants looked on him as the embodi-
ment of the Revolution. He therefore avoided the region where
he had been ill-treated the previous year on his way to Elba and
went instead through friendly territory. On this carefully
selected route, he was greeted with enthusiasm everywhere.
Having quickly forgotten—helped by the reactionary rule of
the Bourbon king—the wars, taxes, boycotts, and casualties of
the Empire, everyone greeted him as if he were the father of his
country, a peaceful ruler outraged about the injustices and the
economic pressures weighing on his people.

Soon Napoleon faced a moment of truth, running into a
detachment of soldiers sent to arrest or even kill him. The
two forces met in a village where the people crowded around
to see what would happen. Napoleon took a bold gamble,
which could easily have cost him his life: he ordered his own
troops to lower their guns. Then he walked toward the government detachment saying, "Soldiers of the Fifth Regiment! Do
you recognize me?"

The officer in charge ordered his men to fire. But no one
moved.

Napoleon resumed walking forward, opened his overcoat,
and called: "If there is any soldier among you who wishes to
kill his Emperor, he may do so. Here I am!"

The government soldiers were stunned. One of them
yelled, *"Vive l'Empereur!"* Others quickly followed suit. They
threw away their weapons and rushed to Napoleon, swearing to
follow him everywhere.

It was an incredible performance, one of Napoleon's
greatest—and riskiest. He had been, as usual, fearless when facing a detachment of soldiers in a military situation, even as he
had been cowardly facing, without troops behind him, a mob
of civilians the year before or in the coup of 1799.

While Napoleon's daring, his dramatic gesture and words
helped, the main cause of his success must have been the state
of popular opinion, which overcame the discipline of the troops.

Word of the incident spread quickly, and when he appeared before the city of Grenoble, the regiment there, led by its colonel, met him and joined him at once. At the head of his growing little army and of thousands of civilian followers, Napoleon entered Grenoble. "Before Grenoble, I was an adventurer; at Grenoble I was a reigning prince." After that, every city on his route joined him. Along the way, he distributed proclamations, printed before he left Elba, promising a new era of peace. His being declared an outlaw by the Fourth Coalition probably confirmed his appeal to the French people.

Meanwhile, back in Paris, the government thought that there would be no problem taking Napoleon prisoner—although they did ready an entire army for that simple task. Napoleon's former generals, whom he had made rich, famous, and aristocratic, fell all over themselves calling him such names as "adventurer" and a "public enemy" who had to be brought back in an iron cage. It was in vain. The tide was going the emperor's way. Bourbon leaders had to flee from hostile civilians and troops in the city of Lyons.

From the time he entered Lyons, Napoleon started acting as the ruler of France. He issued decrees banishing royalists and dismissing officials and legislators not to his liking. On March 19, 1815, Louis XVIII himself fled from Paris, and, on the following day, Napoleon was met by a gigantic cheering crowd as he entered the capital. For the next hundred days, Napoleon was greeted with enthusiasm wherever he went. But this most glorious of his campaigns was only a shooting star in the sky.

Almost everyone wanted to be rid of the Bourbons, but what would be the nature of a new Napoleonic regime? Napoleon was aware that after a year of the corrupt rule of Louis XVIII, France would not put up with a renewal of his own efficient despotism. Glories and wealth such as were carved out by his armies from 1796 to 1812 might create a distraction or a trade-off, but since the losses in 1812, these compensations were no longer available. The enemy had even set foot on French soil. And a new war of invasion was now being proclaimed against Napoleonic France. At the present time he needed less an army of conquest than a civilian population willing to fight to the death at home in France on behalf of a man regarded as an outlaw everywhere else.

As always, he sought the support of the middle class, the men of property and influence who had made the Revolution. They had gotten their voice during the Bourbon restoration after a decade of silence under the Empire, and they could not be silenced again. If they were to fight for him, they needed to have some say in their own destiny. With his usual dexterity, he adapted himself to the changed circumstances and made peace with various liberal opponents. He promised concessions to the party of reform. He would give France the free institutions which, he claimed, adverse circumstances had until now forced him to postpone. He renounced the Grand Empire, which he had been building for sixteen years, in favor of a French Empire. This presumably consisted of "natural" frontiers, liberal institutions and a "constitutional" or limited monarchy.

He gave the task of drafting a progressive constitution to one prominent liberal. The title of this document, "Additional Act to the Constitution of the Empire," revealed that the empire was still primary; its structure was merely being modified somewhat with a few amendments. The new document was modeled on the British and American systems, allowing for a form of popularly elected house of representatives and giving various powers to the legislatures at the expense of the executive. Freedom of expression was emphasized. The head of state would be like the British monarch, above political strife. Hardly Napoleon's style.

The Constitution was proclaimed on June 1, 1815, as part of a large public ceremony harking back to the glorious old days of the coronation of 1804. Napoleon, dressed in coronation robes, made a rousing, if self-contradictory, speech.

Yet these uncharacteristic liberal gestures were not only insincere but useless. They whetted the liberals' appetite for more reforms. If there had been no war, he would have found himself enmeshed in constitutional bickering. Ratified by only a third of the electorate, the document pleased no one, least of all himself. He had always hated democracy, which seemed to him mob rule. The party system and constitutional checks and balances were anarchy to a man who alone knew what was best for everyone. An aristocrat of sorts and a soldier all his life, he was used to giving orders. He would never be the emperor of noisy, demanding radicals with their abstract ideas and system building. On St. Helena years later, he regretted having wasted precious time battling with the liberals over the form of the new constitution when he should have been preparing for war, especially as he would have dismissed the new legislative chambers as soon as he had his first military victory.

Nor did measures like abolishing the slave trade or trying to tempt Talleyrand back into service or informing the czar of a secret treaty between Britain and Austria against Russia do much to impress anyone. The individuals he was catering to with such words knew that he was a man who was played out, as these desperate measures indicated. Still, it must be said, Napoleon now gathered around him a surprisingly good team of ministers—but, alas, too late for France.

For war was inevitable. Even if Napoleon really intended to be a peaceful emperor this time, the allies' understandable distrust left him no choice but to seek a quick military victory to establish himself at least at home. The legislative chambers were told to stick to their knitting while the army took to the field. As in 1800, 1805, 1806, 1809, and 1812, politics and diplomacy awaited the results of war.

Large allied armies were approaching France from every direction. Whether he knew it or not, Napoleon faced desperate odds and the likelihood that any successes would be only temporary stops on the march to defeat. The allies had won the last two big campaigns. Entire French armies had been wiped out. Many French generals had fallen or were no longer loyal to Napoleon. There were defections and defeatism everywhere. France desired peace and liberty. He himself seemed not to be the same man any more. His liberalism appeared improvised and unconvincing. His liberalization of the constitution, its adoption in public, and his instituting the new legislatures all rang false and failed to arouse any enthusiasm. As a proclaimed outlaw, Napoleon would have to defeat Europe singlehandedly, it would seem, to stay in power.

While making some futile attempts to persuade the allies of his peaceful intentions, Napoleon turned his tremendous organizational skills to raising an army. Without conscription, which he dared not reinstitute, he gathered 550,000 men by June 1, although only 230,000 were combat ready and only 130,000 of these were immediately available for his main operations. In contrast to 1814, he now had plenty of veterans, many of them returned prisoners of war.

The allied plan was to begin the offensive with all their forces—some 850,000 men—at once in June. While various allied armies were converging on France, two were already at hand in nearby Belgium, led by the British general Wellington and the Prussian General Blücher. The two generals wanted to attack Napoleon before he was ready. Napoleon took the offensive first, however. He was always lured by a capital—Brussels, in this case—and Belgium was at this time still considered part of France (making Wellington and Blücher invaders). Above all, with a divided, fearful nation behind him, he dared not risk a defensive campaign. He needed a quick, resounding victory over the British and the Prussians in Belgium so as to rally France to his flag, shatter allied unity, and discourage the large Russian and Austrian armies coming from Germany.

Napoleon's strategy was to pretend to be on the defensive, hurry 125,000 troops to the front, attack the allies where they were lightly joined, separate and destroy them by turns. This favorite strategy of his had rarely failed. If the crucial reality in the brief 1815 campaign was allied numerical superiority, it was nearly overcome by Napoleon's acting, as usual, faster than anyone expected.

Napoleon sent one of his generals, Ney, to hold off Wellington at Quatre Bras, while he himself prepared to take on

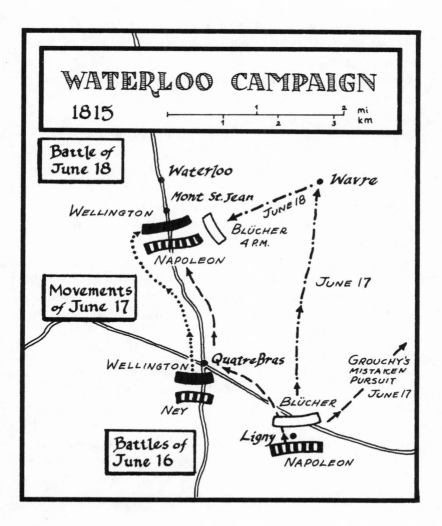

Blücher and the Prussians. As Napoleon started to move, Wellington was slow to respond, so slow in fact that, not expecting any fighting for several days, he did not concentrate his army. He even attended a ball in Brussels and when, at 1.00 A.M., word came of the French threat, he did not leave the ball for another hour.

The first battle took place at Ligny on June 16. Seventy-eight thousand French soldiers attacked eighty-two thousand Prussians. Both sides sustained heavy losses. Because Wellington had not come in time to help Blücher, the French beat the Prussians, though not decisively. The victory would have been bigger, another Jena-Auerstadt, if the attack had started earlier and been better coordinated. Napoleon fell short of crushing Blücher's army because Ney moved a force too slowly, another general, Grouchy, allowed the fleeing Prussians to elude him and reassemble, and a third general marched and countermarched his forces, due to misunderstandings and conflicting orders, without managing to help either the force fighting the Prussians or the one holding off the British. As Napoleon said sarcastically, he "discovered the secret—which seemed beyond human capability—of being" on neither of two simultaneous battlefields.

Napoleon believed that he had now established the sought-after gap between the British and the Prussians. He had taken the advantage in the Belgian campaign and defeated the more difficult of the two adversaries. Now he could turn his attention to Wellington. The Englishman's one hope was to hold on until Blücher could regroup and join him.

On the morning of June 17, it was Napoleon's turn to move too slowly. As a result of excessive optimism, weariness, and sloppy investigation, he concluded that the Prussians were still fleeing. He thought that he had nothing to worry about from Blücher's forces, which were last seen going in three different directions, and that he had plenty of time to annihilate Wellington's forces. Had he attacked Wellington four hours earlier than he did, he would have had a firm numerical superiority and likely a quick victory.

As it turned out, the Prussians did manage to reassemble ninety thousand troops. Blücher, harboring no grudges, was to take them immediately to Wellington's aid. The Englishman was willing to make a stand before Brussels only on receiving Blücher's promise of support. Had Napoleon taken greater care in reconnoitering, he would have seen that the Prussians were preparing to join the battle.

Late in the morning, Napoleon began the attack, the sixtieth and last pitched battle of his career. He was oblivious to the fact that ninety thousand Prussians were within four hours' march. Napoleon had seventy-four thousand excellent troops against Wellington's sixty-eight thousand, who were poorly equipped and staffed, deficient in cavalry and artillery. Before he ordered the main attack, Napoleon heard that the Prussians were on the move. Thinking them to be only forty thousand strong, he placed ten thousand in reserve in case of a Prussian attack. This move made his force numerically inferior to Wellington's.

The battle of Waterloo consisted mainly of a series of tremendous French charges, supported by concentrated artillery fire and repelled by Wellington's troops. In a minor battle in Sicily a few years earlier, a British force of marksmen, holding their ground until they could shoot effectively, defeated a larger French force. Napoleon, who was not there in person and who had never fought British land forces, did not attach any significance to the event and allowed his generals to adhere to standard tactics. Wellington had, however, concluded that the French maneuvers would not work against "steady troops." So now the British marksmen held their ground, and the attempt to break through their lines failed.

The Prussians were drawing closer. Napoleon could still have broken off the engagement as, with each hour, his position became more precarious. But determined to crush the British,

188

*The Battle of Waterloo, as pictured in a British book
of the period.*

he ordered a new attack. Wellington's last reserves just barely beat back two more charges. He held on desperately, knowing that the Prussians were coming.

Wellington paced nervously back and forth in front of the British headquarters tent, looking out into the distance. The sun was setting; whom would it take with it?

"Would God that night or Blücher would come!"

Napoleon paced nervously back and forth at French headquarters.

An officer came with a desperate request that the guard held in reserve be thrown in. Napoleon had been in a similar situation in Borodino. But could he afford to act differently now? Then it had been the fear of being marooned in the middle of barbaric Russia without reserves, without his elite guard. Now it might mean being naked before the onslaught of all Europe. "Troops? Where do you suppose I shall find them? Do you expect me to make them?"

Had a fourth attack been made then, the French might have succeeded. But although his ranks were being thinned, Napoleon, as at Borodino, could not bring himself to throw his last reserve, his guard, into battle. It looked as though the battle would end in a costly French victory or standoff. Both sides waited for the decisive act from outside, the arrival of fresh forces to turn the tide in their favor—the French for Grouchy's thirty thousand men returning from pursuit of the Prussians; the British for what they knew to be ninety thousand Prussians and Napoleon thought to be forty thousand.

Soon after 4:00 P.M., the Prussians appeared at long last. The news of the arrival of ninety thousand Prussians spread through both camps. The British cheered and cracked jokes to relieve the terrible tension that had built up, what with the dead and wounded all about them and the French attack waves seeming endless. The French troops felt a sinking at the heart.

The Prussians had come only just in time, as the French were making a desperate assault. Because Grouchy never showed up—he too managed to be in neither of two concurrent battles —Napoleon finally decided to throw in his last reserves. But Wellington, learning this from a deserter, used every man to hold the front. He managed, with the Prussians in action now, to beat off the French. The guard fell back, the famous, fearsome Napoleonic Guard. Panic seized the weary French, and then a quick retreat turned into a rout, one of the worst collapses in French military history. Napoleon, after failing to stop the rout, barely escaped under cover of members of his guard.

"Never," he later claimed, "did the French army fight better than on that day."

Wellington and Blücher met by chance at the town of Waterloo and exchanged congratulations. They may not have realized at once the military scope of the victory and its political ramifications. Not only were there twenty-five thousand French casualties (against twenty thousand allied ones), but Napoleon himself was beaten.

Once and for all.

Napoleon said on this occasion: "I have but dared too much."

CHAPTER TWELVE

St. Helena
(1815–1821)
and Beyond

N apoleon, so sure of victory, could never account for the defeat. In a detached analysis he made a few years later, he proved how, on the basis of the information available to Wellington, the Englishman made every wrong move possible. But because the information proved incorrect, Wellington won. "Thus the fact—such is the bizarre course of human events!—that the poor choice of his battlefield made all retreat impossible was the cause of his victory." As he had remarked at the end of, and about, the Russian campaign, our enemies' mistakes are the very things that do us in. And that Wellington should win *because* of his ineptness was indeed an irony big enough to match the irony that French numerical superiority in the Russian campaign undid Napoleon.

For his part, Wellington thought that Napoleon erred because of impatience and inability to fight a defensive war.

Waiting was, however, for Napoleon perhaps militarily, and certainly politically, impossible.

In any case, although Waterloo saw many errors and strokes of luck, the ultimate outcome was pretty well determined. It was a decisive battle only in the sense that it marked the end of Napoleon's career, no small thing, to be sure. It was *not* a decisive battle in the sense that it changed history. Napoleon was beaten before it began. Even if he had won at Waterloo, he would have been overwhelmed a few weeks later, for all Europe was aroused, and a million men were closing in on him.

Whether or not his enemy counterparts realized at once the full significance of the battle's outcome, Napoleon did not. Ready to pursue the struggle, he gave orders for a new massing of one hundred fifty thousand troops. He handed the army over to a general and rushed to Paris to organize defenses. But the disaster was vast, and 1815 was not 1812. The public was so alarmed that in less than two days the empire was finished. If in 1814 Talleyrand played a major role in the transition from Napoleon to Louis XVIII, it was now another former key minister of Napoleon's, Fouché, the ex-police chief, who favored a Bourbon restoration. An old politician, adept at switching sides, he had persuaded moderates in 1794 that Robespierre was a dictator who must go. Now he persuaded them that Napoleon was a would-be military dictator who must go.

And indeed those closest to Napoleon urged him to take stern measures in the face of disaster—to form a Dictatorship of Public Salvation. But he refused to "reign by the axe." That left him no options.

Blind faith in the invincible hero was dead in the country at large and certainly in the chamber of the legislature, which was suddenly protected by the national guard. Inside the chamber, the Marquis de Lafayette rose to speak, old, white haired, leathery faced, a little bowed, but as energetic as ever. The "Hero of Two Worlds" had played an important role in the American Revolution. He was a leader in the early phase of the French Revolution. He went into retirement when the later Revolution and the Napoleonic empire became a distortion of all he believed in. This man, whom Napoleon, after trying in vain to buy, had scorned as a mere theorist, a utopian dreamer, and a mule, was elected by admiring fellow Frenchmen as vice-president of the new liberalized legislature.

Always associated with moderation, Lafayette launched the most savage verbal attack that had been heard in France in a long time. An attack on the emperor himself! He ended his speech with a motion: "I therefore hereby solemnly move, Mr. Chairman, that with the nation in the direst peril of its history, this Chamber remain in permanent session [cheers], that any attempt to dissolve this Chamber be declared an act of treason [more cheers], and that the Emperor Napoleon, his empire and his career in shambles, abdicate forthwith!" Cheers, yells, stamping feet, rapping of the gavel, and unanimous approval of the motion by a voice vote: in 1814, the allied armies threw Napoleon out of power; now it was the French people themselves.

Although he might still have had the support of the masses and of the Parisian mobs, Napoleon did not try to dissolve the chambers. Declaring that he did not wish to be an obstacle to peace, he abdicated on June 22 in favor of his son.

The Prussians were hastening to Paris. A provisional government was set up on June 22, with Fouché at its head. It asked Blücher for an armistice now that the emperor had stepped down. Blücher refused to negotiate until Napoleon and the eastern fortresses surrendered. When Blücher tried to kidnap Napoleon with the declared intention of shooting him without a trial, the ex-emperor was sent out of town.

The provisional government proclaimed Napoleon's young son Emperor Napoleon II. For obvious reasons, however, the allies were now more set against any Napoleonic dynasty than they were the year before. The provisional government had to come up with a ruler whom the allies would recognize, before the impulsive Blücher reached Paris, and Blücher was moving very fast. So, for lack of a workable alternative and with the pressure of time, the Bourbons were once more the only choice, the only shield against allied wrath. Wellington had, in any case, already recognized Louis XVIII as king again. On July 3, Blücher was ready to sign an armistice if Paris surrendered, and on July 8, Louis XVIII reentered Paris.

Thus the Hundred Days proved to be a costly detour for France: the most complete rout in the long French military annals; fifty thousand more casualties; a harsher peace treaty than the one of a year before; a large indemnity; a more reactionary restoration. Yet this interlude provided Napoleon with more excitement and the already overloaded Napoleonic saga with more legends. Had he died at Waterloo, charging at the head of his guard, it would have been a glorious, even mythical, end. But as it was, he had yet one more campaign to fight, one not on the military field.

The immediate problem for France was what to do with Napoleon. Clearly finished politically, he remained in the Elysée palace in Paris which he had occupied during the Hundred Days. He was still popular with some of the army and with noisy sections of the populace. There was talk that the army reorganized on the Loire River would receive him with open arms.

For several days, Napoleon lapsed into that recurrent indecisiveness that was as true of him in later years as his more famous dynamism. As in Spain and in Russia, he saw the danger of waiting but could not make up his mind and rouse himself. He expected a favorable turn of events—a split among the allies, a rising of the French people, something else unforeseeable. Finally an order for his arrest reached him. He snuck out to the little château of Malmaison.

Fouché wanted him to go to a port where two boats would take him to America. He spent four days waiting for a safe conduct pass. But the safe conduct to the United States—that haven for people wanting to make a fresh start in life—was refused.

Napoleon now had the gall to offer his services as "General Bonaparte" to the provisional government—as though everyone could simply return to 1796 and to the Italian campaign of the loyal general of the republic. After all he had proved about himself since then, would not the rest of the cycle repeat itself? And, knowing that, would the allies put up with the idea for one moment? Naturally the provisional government rejected him at once. It wanted him out of the country.

He then asked to be allowed to settle for good in Britain—the land of the people he most hated and who were his most enduring enemy. This was another pipe dream, originating in the fact that one of his brothers and, long ago, his former hero, General Paoli, had lived there contentedly for years as British squires. It was too good to be true for Napoleon. The conservative British government was on shaky political ground at home. It was aware of pro-French-Revolutionary sentiments among the populace and the intellectuals. It was not about to have a magnetic personality like Napoleon on hand somewhere in the outskirts of London.

The problem was, where do you store a bag of dynamite? The allies were also wondering what to do with him. Elba had proved to be a failure. Everyone therefore returned to an idea already broached at the Congress of Vienna, of interning him on a remote island that belonged to Britain, St. Helena. The allies, declaring Napoleon their prisoner, with Britain responsible for his confinement, therefore, turned him over to the British. On July 15, he had himself rowed to a British ship and placed under the protection of the British ruler and laws. "I come, like Themistocles, to claim a seat by the hearth of the British people." He only just missed being handed over to the French government to be shot.

On July 31, the British, acting for the allies, deported him to St. Helena. He was treated as a retired general, not as an ex-emperor, and Napoleon, who considered himself a guest rather than a prisoner of the British, deeply resented this insult. He would have been even more insulted had he known that on board the ship he seemed to British officers to be fat and mediocre-looking, not at all a "great or extraordinary man."

On October 15, 1815, Napoleon, accompanied by a few followers, came to St. Helena, a small island in the middle of the Atlantic used as a refueling and resupply station for ships making the journey between Britain and India. He settled briefly in a small house, where he spent the most carefree days of his captivity, probably of his life. He started to dictate the story of his career, took long leisurely walks, and struck up a good-natured friendship with the thirteen-year-old daughter of the British family he stayed with. The latter brought out the human side of his nature. How many schoolgirls get a chance to practice their French lessons with a real French emperor and to have the great Napoleon as a tutor for their history homework?

Two months later, he moved into a somewhat larger country residence, where he spent the rest of his life. He who had hurried all his life from one part of Europe to another, lived in splendid palaces in great capital cities, and seldom stayed anywhere longer than four weeks at a time now was to spend six years in a few small, crowded rooms of a one-story house. On Corsica, he had been a native and a noble; on Elba, a sovereign ruler; but here, on his third island, he was a prisoner, St. Helena a fort, the governor a jailer. Still insisting on being the guest, not the prisoner, of Britain, he threw himself into the role of being a martyr.

He continued dictating the story of his career, sometimes for fourteen hours at a stretch. Although he was a master at organizing men and a master at organizing words, he curiously lacked the literary skills necessary for memoirs. Since the person writing it all down was similarly untalented, the memoirs remain fragmentary and unimpressive. Yet they contain many

Some of the furniture from Napoleon's room at St. Helena. The portrait is presumably that of his son, Napoleon II. On the lower left is the controversial plaster cast of his face after death.

fascinating glimpses of his mind and reveal how he thought, at least in looking back, about his experiences. Napoleon was, it should be realized, one of the few great men of history to go into retirement—in his case, forced retirement. Alexander,

Caesar, and most of the rest died prematurely or in office, taking the secrets of their careers and goals with them. Retirement means time for reflection, for commenting on what might or should have been. It means giving the final, rounded view of one's intentions and experiences rather than the half-formed and unexpressed ones one has in the haste of action. Napoleon had many comments to make.

Like his last will and his conversations with those around him in exile (which he knew would be transcribed and published), the dictated memoirs tell the world what he wanted it to hear. His purpose was to impress on posterity the legend that the Napoleonic Empire was founded on the principles of liberalism, pacifism, nationalism, and religious tolerance and that Napoleon, as champion of the Revolutionary principles of 1789, had the noblest of ambitions: to establish "at last the kingdom of reason and the full exercise, the complete enjoyment, of all human capabilities!" It was only because of the malevolence of the reactionary great powers and the circumstances of the hour that he was forced to defend his regime and to preserve the Revolution by means of wars and harsh measures. Only inadvertently did he become the conqueror of Europe and the founder of a universal monarchy. "The world begged me to govern it; sovereigns and nations vied with one another in throwing themselves under my scepter."

That thesis is what historians call the Napoleonic gospel of St. Helena. Its recasting of his own character and reign was therefore his last and greatest campaign, what one historian amusingly calls "a wheeling movement of incredible daring, his strategic masterpiece, his most outstanding victory—a victory wrenched out of utter defeat." Whether you believe Napoleon or not—whether he at last had the chance to reveal to the world the secret of his misunderstood career or whether he only now discovered or invented after the fact a nobler, altruistic purpose to all his mindless activism—there was a truth to his words: "My downfall raises me to infinite heights."

Looking back, however, could not compensate for his present indignities. He could not adjust to the idea of being a captive. He resented the fact that a British officer always accompanied him on his walks. He would have had another complaint if he had known that his Irish doctor was a double agent. He resented the British addressing him as "General Bonaparte" and withholding recognition of him as the Emperor Napoleon. Insisting on being called emperor and keeping up the ritual of a court was saying that his career and regime, which now seemed remote and dreamlike, had actually occurred.

Things worsened when in April 1816, Sir Hudson Lowe, a pedantic, suspicious man who quarreled with everyone, was appointed governor of St. Helena's. As one historian nicely puts it, one who knew only how to command was the prisoner of one who knew only how to obey. The two men took an intense dislike to each other, and there were frequent quarrels over utter trivia. Lowe cut down Napoleon's privileges. There were also quarrels among Napoleon's followers, and the one feeling that became uppermost through the days and years was boredom.

The times when Napoleon dreamed of a return, when he thought that he might be needed to stop the royalist oppression of the people, to keep the radicals in line, or force the other nations to respect France, grew fewer and further apart. He may have had some hopes for his son, but the son was being brought up in Austria as a Germanic prince, with little awareness of being a Frenchman, a Bonaparte, or the great Napoleon's offspring. Napoleon's wife was too preoccupied with another man to care about the son. Only Napoleon's mother was sure that her grandson's hour would come and that he would yet ascend to the throne of France. But in fact, the son, coming to admire his father and to be ashamed of his mother, died young.

Napoleon gradually became reclusive, spending long hours in bed or bath. He was growing more bored, tired, and, finally, ill. He gave up any thoughts of a recall. He who in his prime almost always had awakened looking forward to achieving some gigantic thing that day, as hardly anyone else ever had, now had nothing at all to look forward to.

In 1817, he began to suffer from indigestion, swelling of the legs, loss of appetite, and insomnia. He was diagnosed as having hepatitis (inflammation of the liver) and treated with mercury. As the quarrels among jealous rivals for his affection increased, some either gave up and left or were dismissed by the British. Charges and countercharges were made by them as to whether Napoleon was sick or only feigning it, whether the British were treating or mistreating him. As a result, for one period of eight months, he received no medical attention at all.

The hopes he harbored for at least a release from St. Helena ended in 1818, when the allies reaffirmed the conditions of his detention. Several prominent people, including the same pope he had once harassed, kidnapped, and put into solitary confinement, interceded in vain on his behalf. Escape from St. Helena was far more difficult than from Elba and probably never seriously considered by him.

On June 16, 1819, he suffered a stroke. For a while in 1819–20, he recovered enough to immerse himself in an elaborate gardening project. Here was the former emperor of Europe, in dirty work shirt and pants and in muddy boots, digging with a homely shovel in order to sow seeds, plant bushes, move flowers—even as he used to make millions of soldiers dig fortifications that spanned a continent. Roses were now his soldiers, a garden his empire, an island his universe.

Then his health declined again. Life became even more lonely and boring. He worsened in late 1820. In April 1821, he became very ill, and a newly arrived British doctor diagnosed cancer of the stomach. Although weak, he drafted a long will in which he disposed of all his possessions and took care of all his relatives and friends.

On his deathbed, he seemed to mutter, "France . . . army . . . head of the army . . . Josephine. . . ." As his entourage sat around him in a vigil, he died at 6:00 P.M. on May 5, 1821, in the fifty-second year of his life. Outside, an Atlantic storm raged.

An autopsy established the cause of death as cancer of the stomach. Yet Napoleon remained controversial to the end and even beyond. There were then, and have been since, many charges and countercharges over the actual cause of death, over the autopsy itself, over whether his liver was unusually large though normal or abnormally enlarged, over whether he was poisoned (by the British?), over whether the diagnosis of cancer of the stomach, the same disease that killed his father, was reliable or merely a convenient excuse made up by the British. There have even been controversies about how authentic the death mask allegedly taken of him is.

The French theory is that Napoleon died of a disease of the liver brought on by the climate of St. Helena. The British theory is that the symptoms were hypochrondriacal or, if real, due to a genetically caused cancer. No one diagnosed in time a gastric ulcer he had apparently long had, and one should not rule out a psychosomatic factor. Someone with his temperament and career, deprived of activity, interest, and hope, may well have died of despair and frustration, of the sheer absence of something to live for or look forward to. He himself said, "It would surely be better to die than go on vegetating here as I have done for the last six years." And: "I was Napoleon then; today I am nothing. . . . I vegetate, I no longer live." A death in Moscow or during a charge at Waterloo would certainly have better fitted his career than this gradual decline into triviality, indignity, illness, and barren controversy.

The British refused to allow his body to be taken to France, and he was buried between two trees that he particularly enjoyed. His will expressed the desire to rest on the banks of the Seine "in the midst of the people I so greatly loved." It was not until 1840 that popular opinion, under the sway of nostalgia for a by-now heavily romanticized Napoleon, forced Louis Philippe, the current king, to have his coffin brought to Paris and placed in the Invalides amid tremendous crowds and splendid ceremonies.

Napoleon's tomb in the Invalides in Paris.

Ultimately his military and political achievements don't matter to us as much as does the question of who or what he was. Most people when young dream of greatness, of being superman, of being able to order others around, of being all-powerful, immortal, godlike, and famous. As we grow up, we put such dreams aside and learn to settle for mortality, normality, obscurity, even mediocrity. Napoleon was one of the very few who never put that dream aside but worked all his life to make it real. That dream that most children have of proving themselves some day was fulfilled by Napoleon as by no one else. As he said to one of his brothers at the time of his coronation as emperor: "If only our father could see us now."

That sad little boy in snowy Autun came closer than anyone to making his dream real because he had the rare combination of extraordinary intelligence, imagination, energy, charm, determination, flexibility, quickness, and, not least, luck. Often Napoleon realized that the stakes in his life were very high, that he was close to having "the greatest reputation that has ever existed," to being "the greatest man known to history."

But even such rare achievements have their limits. Men fall short of being gods, although they sometimes forget it when things go well. It was Napoleon's mother who said, at the time of her son's zenith, when her once semiobscure and foreign family was ruling France and most of Europe as no other family ever had, *"Pourvu que cela dure!"* "If only it would last!" That can be said of everyone's life and achievements, of the human race itself. So it was that when informed of Napoleon's death, the wily Talleyrand—who had conceded that the Napoleon he had betrayed and called uncivilized was an "extraordinary" man —said: "An event? Hardly. Just an item of news."

"Pourvu que cela dure!"

Nothing lasts.

That is the ultimate meaning of the life of the man who was perhaps the greatest man of action in history, one of a handful of supreme geniuses, who was on the cutting edge of experience, who was an astronaut of both good and evil accomplishments, whose motives are at once as clear as glass and as mysterious as death, and who was the superman of our dreams —Napoleon Bonaparte.

Further Reading

Butterfield, Herbert. *Napoleon*. New York: Macmillan, 1956.

Fisher, H.A.L. *Napoleon*. London: Oxford University Press, 1912.

Guérard, Albert. *Napoleon I*. New York: Alfred Knopf, 1962.

Herold, J. Christopher. *The Mind of Napoleon*. New York: Columbia University Press, 1955.

Kircheisen, F.M. *Napoleon*, translated by Henry St. Lawrence. New York: Harcourt Brace, 1932.

Markham, Felix. *Napoleon*. New York: New American Library, 1963.

Thompson, J.M. *Napoleon Bonaparte*. New York: Oxford University Press, 1952.

Index

A

Aboukir, 43, 45, 158
Acre, 45
Africa, 40
Ajaccio, 7, 18
Alexander I, Czar of Russia, 82, 86,
    94, 96–98, 100, 112–13, 133–39,
    146–47, 154, 164, 171–75
Alexander the Great, 35, 38, 42, 112,
    134, 198
Alexandria, 39, 45–46
Alps Mountains, 35, 63, 113
America, 59, 68, 182, 195
American Revolution, 194
Amiens Treaty, 64–65, 78, 156
Antwerp, 122, 165
Arcole, 30, 32, 65

Army of England, 38
Army of the Interior, 26
Army of Italy, 23, 26–27, 37–39, 86
Army of the Rhine, 31
artillery, 23, 121, 187
Asia, 45
Aspern-Essling, 120, 122
Atlantic, 197, 202
Auerstadt, 94, 186
Austerlitz, 86, 88, 98, 107, 113–15,
    154
Austria, 23, 28, 30–33, 35–36, 38, 45,
    49, 62–64, 72, 76, 82–83, 86, 88,
    90–91, 94–95, 103, 107–08, 112–24,
    126–28, 134, 160–63, 168–71, 176,
    179, 183–84, 200–01
Autun, 5, 8

INDEX

B

Baílen, 107, 119, 130
Baltic Sea, 90
Bank of France, 58
Battle of Nations, 164
Bautzen, 162
Bavaria, 83, 165
Beethoven, 67
Belgium, 127, 167, 184
Berezina River, 153, 164
Berlin, 92–94, 145, 147
Blücher, Gen., 100, 184–87, 190–91,
  194–95
Bonaparte, Josephine de
  Beauharnais, 26, 73, 123, 201
Bordeaux, 171
Borodino, 142, 144, 152, 190
Bourbon, House of, 21, 49, 55, 64,
  66, 69, 71, 104, 116, 119, 122, 124,
  127, 167, 178, 180–82, 193, 195
Brienne, 9–10
Britain, 21–23, 28, 38, 42–49, 67–69,
  78–83, 90–91, 95, 98–99, 101, 103,
  107–110, 119–22, 126–35, 162–65,
  168–71, 179, 182–90, 196–97,
  200–02. *See also* England.
Brussels, 184–87
Buonaparte, Carlo, 7–8, 202
Buonaparte, Joseph, 10, 90, 104–5,
  171
Buonaparte, Letizia, 7–8, 75, 177,
  200, 204
Buonaparte, Louis, 127
Buonaparte, Lucien, 49–51
Byron, 67–68

C

Caesar, Julius, 35, 39, 47, 60–61, 199
Cairo, 39, 42–45, 108
Cannes, 179

Caribbean, 80
Carnot, 52
Catholic Church, 56–59, 62, 65,
  71–73, 76, 101, 104, 105, 110–12,
  156
Channel, 80, 126
Charlemagne, 76, 112
Charles, Archduke, 32, 119
Cisalpine Republic, 33, 64
Comédie Française, 148
Concordat of 1801–2, 56, 64–65, 70,
  110, 112, 156
Confederation of the Rhine, 90,
  127, 160, 165
Congress of Vienna, 179, 196
Constantine, 112
Constantinople, 45, 133
Continental System, 91, 99–104, 107,
  110–11, 127–29, 133
Copenhagen, 103
Corsica, 6–11, 14–20, 23, 26–27, 36,
  124, 176, 197
Cossacks, 149, 153
Council of Ancients, 48, 50
Council of Five Hundred, 48–51,
  53
Cromwell, Oliver, 60
Crusades, 39, 46

D

Damascus, 44
Dante, 153
Danton, 52
Danube, 82, 88
Dardanelles, 133
Denmark, 103
Directory, 24, 27, 29, 35–39, 46–51,
  61, 86, 179
Divan, 40
Dresden, 136, 163–64

E

Eckmuhl, 120

Egypt, 38–39, 42–49, 65, 78–82, 104, 134, 149, 156, 158, 176, 179

Elba, 176–81, 196–97, 201

Elysée Palace, 195

d'Enghien, Duke, 71

England, 14, 18, 59, 62, 192. *See also* Britain.

Erfurt, 112–13, 137

Europe, 35, 38, 46, 60, 64–65, 68–72, 78, 82, 91, 95, 98, 100–01, 103, 107, 110–17, 123, 127, 130, 132–35, 156, 158, 160, 163, 166, 170, 175–76, 187, 190, 193, 197, 201, 204

Eylau (Preussisch), 95, 144

F

Fontainebleau, Palace of, 112, 172, 176

Fouché, 102, 108, 193–95

Fourth Coalition, 162, 179, 181

Francis I, Emperor of Austria, 31–32 82, 86, 116, 124, 161, 164

Frederick the Great, King of Prussia, 95, 175

Frederick William, King of Prussia, 91, 164, 171

Fréjus, 176

French Revolution, 15, 20–21, 27, 33, 36–40, 52–56, 59–60, 64, 66, 68, 70–71, 79–80, 91, 101, 104, 116–17, 124, 129, 159, 165–66, 172, 178, 180, 182, 194, 196, 199

Friedland, 95, 98

G

Ganges River, 134

Genoa, 8, 36, 63

Germany, 31, 90, 107, 116, 122, 129, 134, 139, 157, 159, 166–67, 176, 184. *See also* Prussia.

Gibraltar, 39, 117

Gizeh, 39

God, 56, 65, 101, 112, 138, 154, 190

Grand Army, 82, 86, 94, 120, 126, 130, 135, 137, 144, 153–56, 159, 169

Greek Tragedy, 100

Grenoble, 181

Grouchy, Gen., 186, 190

H

Hamburg, 100

Hapsburg, House of, 76, 119, 160

Heilsberg, 95

Hitler, 133

Holland, 72, 127–28, 165

Holy Roman Empire, 76, 82, 90

Hundred Days, 175, 181, 195

I

India, 38, 43, 98, 134, 197

Industrial Revolution, 128

infantry, 23, 187

Institute of Egypt, 42

Institute of France, 38, 49

Invalides, 203

Islam, 41

Italy, 23, 27, 29, 31–38, 45–49, 63–65, 71, 76, 81–82, 86, 88, 90, 104, 107, 110–13, 118, 122, 127, 134, 139, 169, 176–77, 196

J

Jacobins, 49, 54

Jaffa, 43–44

Jena, 94, 98, 186

K

Königsberg, 95
Kovno, 156
Kremlin, 137–39, 146–49, 156
Kutuzov, Gen., 136, 140–44, 149,
    152–53, 160

L

Lafayette, Marquis de, 52, 68,
    193–94
La Rothière, 167
Legion of Honor, 55–57
Leipzig, 161–64
liberty, 66–67, 117–18, 123, 129, 165,
    182
Ligny, 186
Lisbon, 104, 108, 130
Lodi, 31, 64
Loire River, 195
Lombardy, 31, 63, 76
London, 80, 196
Louis XIV, 58, 60, 175
Louis XVI, 17, 21, 23, 124, 174
Louis XVIII, 64–65, 174, 178, 181,
    193, 195
Louis Philippe, 203
Low Countries, 90, 127, 165
Lowe, Sir Hudson, 200
Lunéville Treaty, 64
Lützen, 162
Lyons, 181

M

Mack, Gen., 83–85, 94, 136
Madrid, 104–05, 108, 142, 145–47,
    162
Malmaison Castle, 195
Malta, 39, 78
Mamelukes, 42
Mantua, 31–32

Marat, 52
Marengo, 63–64, 83, 98
Maria Theresa, Queen of Austria,
    124
Marie Antoinette, Queen of France,
    14, 124
Marie Louise, Princess, 124–26, 176
Marne River, 169
Marseilles, 21, 26
Masséna, Gen., 130
Mecca, 42
Mediterranean Sea, 7, 21, 42–43, 176
Middle East, 38
Milan, 31, 36, 76, 110
Minsk, 153
Mirabeau, Count, 52
Mohammed, 42
Montgolfier brothers, 127
Moscow, 132, 137–49, 154, 156–59,
    164, 202
Moslem, 40–41
Mount Tabor, 44

N

Naples, 45, 72, 88, 127, 165
Napoleon II, King of Rome, 126,
    152, 172, 194, 198, 200
Napoleonic Civil Code, 59, 62, 117
Napoleonic (or Grand) Empire,
    66–76, 80, 88–90, 107, 115–18,
    126–27, 157–60, 182, 199
nationalism, 105–08, 117, 122, 159
Nelson, Admiral, 43, 80, 82
Ney, Gen., 185
Niemen River, 96–98, 137
North Sea, 90
Notre Dame Cathedral, 73, 156

O

Ottoman Empire, 42

P

Palestine, 43, 46
Paoli, Pasquale, 8, 17–18, 196
Papal States, 110
Paris, 9, 15, 23–24, 26, 29, 35–39,
    46–52, 59, 63, 69–70, 108, 111–12,
    119, 129, 148, 152, 155–58, 165,
    167–72, 178–81, 193–95, 202–03
Parliament, 127
Peninsular War, 107, 129–30
Persia, 95
Petersburg, 148
Piedmont, 28–29, 64
Pius VII, Pope, 110–12, 123, 172,
    201
Poles, 95
Pomerania, 135
Portugal, 103–4, 107, 122, 126,
    129–33
Pressburg Treaty, 88, 116
Prussia, 83, 86, 90–91, 94–95, 99,
    103, 107, 112, 119–22, 130, 134,
    136, 147, 158–60, 163, 167–71,
    179, 186–87, 190–91, 194. *See also*
    Germany.
Pyrenees Mountains, 35, 107, 113

Q

Quatre Bras, 185

R

Reign of Terror, 26
Revolution of 1789, *see* French
    Revolution
Rhine River, 31, 35, 45, 83, 113, 160,
    165, 167
Rhodes, 45
Riga, 152
Rivoli, 32
Robespierre, 23, 52, 193

Romantic, 67
Rome, 38, 47, 51, 56, 98, 100,
    110–11, 126
Rosetta Stone, 42
Royalists, 37
Russia, 32, 45–46, 49, 82–83, 86, 88,
    91, 94–95, 98–101, 103, 107–08,
    110, 113, 119–29, 132–63, 166–71,
    179, 183–84, 190, 192, 195

S

Salamanca, 108, 130, 142
St. Helena, 156, 183, 192, 196–202
Schönbrunn Treaty, 122
Seine River, 169, 202
Sicily, 187
Smolensk, 140–41, 148, 152–53
Spain, 21, 72, 80–82, 90, 101, 104–22,
    126–36, 142, 144, 147, 149, 154,
    156–59, 162, 165, 167, 176, 195
Suez Canal, 42
Sweden, 135
Switzerland, 64, 83, 104, 127, 167
Syria, 43–44, 149

T

Talleyrand, 100, 102, 108, 160,
    171–72, 178, 183, 193, 204
Themistocles, 196
Third Coalition, 66, 76, 83, 88
Tilsit, 96–101, 112–13, 116, 133
Toulon, 21–24
Toulouse, 131
Trafalgar, 82
Tuileries Palace, 52, 156, 158, 167
Turks, 42–45, 95, 99, 133
Tyrol, 83, 107, 122, 147

U

Ulm, 83–86, 91
University of France, 58, 62

INDEX

V

Vatican, 56
Venice, 36
Vienna, 32, 38, 67, 83, 86–88, 120,
   145, 147
Vilna, 137–39, 149, 156
Vitebsk, 139, 149
Vitoria, 131, 162

W

Wagram, 121–22, 128
Warsaw, 95

Washington, George, 67–68
Waterloo, 185, 187–93, 195, 202
Wellesley, Arthur, Duke of
   Wellington, 100, 107, 129–30, 136,
   142, 162, 170, 184–87, 190–92,
   195
West Indies, 26
Westphalia, 90
Würmser, Count, 32

Y

Young Guard, 144, 155, 190–91